Knock,

who was there?

A brief history of

Knock, Belmont & Strandtown

and the people who lived there

Keith Haines

BALLYHAY BOOKS

First published by Ballyhay Books,
an imprint of Laurel Cottage Ltd.
Ballyhay, Donaghadee, N. Ireland 2014.

Design & origination in N. Ireland.
Printed & bound in Europe
ISBN 978 1 900935 89 0

This work is dedicated to a great friend and survivor
and stalwart of the East Belfast community,
Ted Cooke

who has graced the MCC,
coached Irish cricketers,
won the Burney Cup,
yet still found time to teach the Professor of Modern
and Medieval German Studies
at Cambridge University

who adds this sentiment of Otto von Bismarck:

*Ein bißchen Freundschaft ist mir mehr Wert als die
Bewunderung der ganzen Welt.*
(A little friendship is worth more to me than the admiration of the whole world).

CONTENTS

A Brief History of the Greater Knock Area

The Naming Of Knock

Whether or not Columba, the irascible sixth-century Irish saint, ever graced the Knock district is impossible to prove, but it is plausible, and it was his name which was a key part in the naming of the area some 1000 years after his death.

Columba (or Columcille, as he was known to the Irish) was a senior figure in the O'Neill clan in the 6th century and, although a monk, was by most accounts strong willed and ill tempered, embodying the arrogance and the tempestuous, imperious character of the O'Neill clan. Having made many enemies at home, like so many of his fellow countrymen since, he sought spiritual renewal in pastures new, but his memory remained cherished in his homeland.

In the succeeding millennium the fortunes of the O'Neill clan waxed and waned but by the 14th and 15th centuries, after the intrusion of the Anglo-French invaders led by John de Courcy, their fortunes were again on the rise, particularly in south Antrim (which became known as Lower Clandeboye) and north Down (or

Upper Clandeboye). Seeking to consolidate their restored authority as Gaelic lords, they sought justification from the past by drawing attention to their connection to their popular distant clansman in the hope that his reputation would rub off on them. As part of this campaign the clan made generous donations to one of their spiritual centres, the historic church on the hill (or *Cnoc*, in Irish) with the result that by 1605 Columba's name had become inextricably associated with the church and the wider district which, as both a parish and a townland, had become identified as Knockcolumcille.

By the early 17th century this church, sited at what is now the junction of the Knock dual carriageway and the Sandown Road, along with the creation of a castle near the top of what is today Church Road in Castlereagh had seemingly cemented the authority of the O'Neills in Upper Clandeboye but this was not to be.

Half a century later their power had been greatly diminished and Columcille's name was not in favour with the new ruling classes on his journey to Movilla; the district became more popularly referred to as Knock, by which name it has been since known.

Stretching the Boundary

The site of Knock(columcille) rises roughly at the centre of the locality covered by this book. This stretches eastwards to incorporate the present-day districts of Knock, Belmont, Sydenham and Strandtown (the last three all being, probably significantly, non-Gaelic names), southwards towards Dundonald, and westwards towards Cregagh and Knockbreda. Whilst the choice of such boundaries is subjective, there are sound historical reasons for such a broad focus.

Lines of burial mounds, mottes, fortifications and other prominent geographical points converge on Knock. The historic path which Columba may have taken on his journey to Movilla probably ran along the brow of the Castlereagh hills – on which the O'Neills built their castle – which overlooked the ancient wooded plain whose early character is retained in such townland names as Ballyrushboy (*Baile Ros Buí*: townland of the yellow woods), now bisected by the lower Castlereagh Road.

Even in the 19th century, the district tended to retain its all-embracing character: in the 1865-1866 *Belfast & Ulster Street Directory*, 'Knock' encompasses Summerfield at Dundonald (now effectively Knock Golf Club), Thornhill (close to the current Knock junction), Knock House (adjacent to the historic graveyard on the mound), Glenview (just above the Castlereagh junction), in addition to the rather more distant Cregagh. Also, as the residential aspect of the district gathered momentum, addresses listed in the *Directory* at Belmont also included those which today would be distinctly located in Strandtown, Sydenham and even Dundonald, in addition to Knock.

Medieval Knock

There are few surviving substantive memorials to the early inhabitants of Knock. These are limited to a series of megaliths or standing stones around Dundonald – the most notable being the Longstone, plus the remains of raths and ancient burial grounds as at Dundonald, Gortgrib and Belvoir Park.

To some extent this is conjecture, but archaeological evidence reveals that the location had been inhabited intermittently from the Mesolithic period to the Bronze Age. It is not unreasonable to speculate that, throughout the early medieval era, the fame and international reputation of Movilla – and its neighbour, Bangor Abbey (founded by St Comgall in 558) – generated much through traffic.

Between the 9th and 12th centuries, although specific information is scarce, Knock endured instability and uncertainty. The historic coastal monasteries were the major institutions and foci of economic activity in the area. It is impossible to make a realistic assessment of their population at this time. They were much more substantial than the pictorial representations often imply, which would have had little appeal to rapacious raiders. Alternatively, the assertion – blithely repeated – that Bangor Abbey hosted a monastic population of several thousand is certainly a medieval exaggeration.

The district suffered the reverberations of the Viking incursions, which commenced at the end of the 8th century. Bangor and Movilla were attacked at least twice between 823 and 825, and at intervals thereafter; from around 840 onwards the Vikings also conducted more inland raids. This period appears to have witnessed a certain discouragement to and decline of monastic life in the lower Ards as, by 973, Bangor and Movilla were governed by a common abbot and the situation was to change even more radically half a century later with the arrival in Ireland of the (so-called) Normans.

In the early medieval era the inhabitants of Knock – or, more broadly, the north Down area – were content to pursue privately the routine of daily life or the rumpus of local, tribal warfare. From the end of the 8th century, however, outsiders began to take an interest in their locality and thereafter the misery, depredation and exploitation endured intermittently until the early 17th century – as in Ireland as a whole – was generally blamed upon English neighbours – at least until the term 'British' gained currency following the Acts of Union. This singular attribution is, however, misleading and erroneous.

Invaders

The earliest medieval invaders were Scandinavian. In 1315, for three years, and more enduringly from the early 17th century, the intruders and settlers were primarily Scottish. Only perhaps in the last quarter of the 16th century, with Sir Thomas Smith's arrival in north Down, can the interlopers be defined as English.

In 1169 others had landed in Co Wexford from England, and more were to follow during the next two years, including the king of England, Henry II. The chronicler Gerald of Wales described these events as *adventus Anglorum*: the arrival of the English. He was, however, incorrect. From 1066 until the reign of John (1199-1216) the primary focus of all the kings of England was their extensive French territories – such as Normandy, Aquitaine and Anjou – and their language was French; it was a historical accident that England happened to be their fortuitous, wealthy acquisition. The invaders who eventually came north to be the new masters of the kingdom of Ulaid (effectively counties Antrim and Down) bore indisputably French names: John de Courcy and Hugh de Lacy.

It is also a strange, but singular truth that these ambitious men are universally referred to as Normans or Anglo-Normans. It has become a convenient shorthand – but it is untrue as they were from a dynasty which succeeded the Normans. To describe them as Normans is no more accurate than describing the men who fought in the First World War as Victorians. Henry II (1154-1189), the instigator of the Plantagenet dynasty which ruled England until 1485, was an Angevin, a dynasty who were apparently not held in particularly high esteem in their own lands if we are to believe to Gerald of Wales; they were regarded by St Bernard of Clairvaux (a leading French bishop and the Cistercian sponsor of St Malachy) as "the Devil's brood".

The Angevins

Research has convincingly revealed that John de Courcy's invasion of Co Down in 1177 was not rash or spontaneous, but a sanguine and optimistic engagement which succeeded as a result of:

> *long-term planning and a shrewd understanding of the political ground-rules of the region ...*

It was the foreigners who first envisaged, in the last quarter of the 12th century, the economic and political potential of the Knock district and its hinterland. Many of the native Irish had occupied the raths, "usually constructed", in Sean Duffy's words, "in places where the land was worth farming". Whilst there were a substantial number in the Castlereagh hills, they were not numerous in the vicinity of Ards and north Down, possibly because of the authority exercised by the principal monasteries. Commentators state that it was at this time that the prosperity of eastern Ulster first becomes apparent, as the invaders and settlers "brought a wholly different concept of lordship to Ireland, which rested on new ideas of land organisation and how best to exploit the power and wealth which accrued from its possession". The increased exploitation of the region's fertility may also have owed some debt to the fortuitous coincidence of a climatic improvement lasting for just over a century leading to increase agricultural output right across Europe, about the time of the arrival of de Courcy.

The chronicler Gerald of Wales suggests that de Courcy's efforts were not without difficulty, but that ultimately they proved very profitable: "He fortified all parts of Ulaid with castles built in suitable places and – not without a great deal of toil, short rations and endurance and many dangers – settled it and established conditions of the utmost peace and stability".

Although it was introduced only in the late 12th and early 13th centuries, de Courcy imposed and entrenched his authority in the

Knock district by means of the erection of the standard Norman structure – the motte. The fact that five were built in the vicinity – at Holywood, Ballymaghan, Dundonald and Belvoir, as well as at Knock itself – is a clear indication of the strategic importance and economic priority of the area, and probably reflects the existence of (in contemporary terms) a sizeable population.

To reinforce his hold on the area, de Courcy imported from the west coast of Scotland and England peasant farmers, parish priests, burgesses, artisans and labourers, and imposed the administrative framework and machinery which had served the Normans well in England. The conquered land was subdivided into manors, some of which became substantial; the most significant in the Knock district was Dundonald.

The Scots and the Demise of the Angevins

The contemporary Knock and north Ards region enjoyed a period of relative peace for thirty years until 1315, but events conspired to drag the locality into affairs across the Irish Sea. Edward I (1272-1307), one of whose nicknames was Hammer of the Scots, proved determined to consolidate his authority over the Welsh and Scottish princes, and his campaigns against the latter between 1295 and 1302 were to cast a lengthy and disturbing shadow across the narrow stretch of water separating Ulster and Scotland.

The leading Scottish nobleman, Robert Bruce, was descended from the Irish Gaelic aristocracy and, in 1302, he consolidated this relationship by his marriage to the daughter of the second Earl of Ulster. As a result of King Edward's success in Scotland, Robert sought respite and solace on the western shore of the Irish Sea (where legend claims that he watched the spider on Rathlin island), and counties Antrim and Down became reluctantly embroiled in Scottish affairs.

Edward Bruce (Robert's younger brother) styled himself King of Ireland and landed at Larne in May 1315 with 6000 men. Carrickfergus was, however, unsympathetic to his aspirations and those who occupied the gentle slopes on the northern Co. Down littoral cannot have been oblivious to the progress of a siege which lasted until September 1316. Until Edward Bruce died in October 1318, the Knock district witnessed and experienced unnerving and calamitous circumstances, primarily because the Scottish presence in Ireland coincided with climatic changes which triggered a terrible famine afflicting much of northern Europe.

Occupying armies always place intolerable pressure upon a regional economy, but in these years of bitter winters, wet summers and failed crops, the inhabitants of north Down were barely able to feed themselves, let alone cater for voracious interlopers who probably used the locality as a base camp. One historian is probably accurate in his summary when he says that the period 1315-1318 "did incalculable damage to the cause of peace and prosperity in Ireland, and has rightly been regarded as the turning-point of English influence ... Ulster in particular, the headquarters of Bruce's army, was utterly devastated and denuded of food and underwent all the horrors of acute famine".

At an enquiry held on 27 September 1333 witnesses offered a bleak insight into the devastation visited upon the district. In many instances the valuation of a locality had been greatly reduced; they revealed that at Dundonald manor "there are seven acres of land and pasture which used to be let to farm for 4 shillings, but are now worth nothing on account of the destruction of war and want of tenants". Except for a watermill, now assessed at half its previous value "on account of the war", there were no buildings remaining in Dundonald, but "there was a castle which is now prostrate and destroyed by the War of the Scots".

The O'Neills (Uí Neill)

The economic hardship visited upon the wider Knock region in the first half of the 14th century was compounded by the consequences of the Black Death which ravaged Ireland in the late 1340s. Whilst it is difficult to be precise about what happened in the north Down locality, it cannot have remained immune from the economic decline of the period.

By the mid-15th century the O'Neills were entrenched. Nevertheless, whatever gratification and nostalgia may have been evoked by a return to a traditional Gaelic life-style and law, it presented one principal disadvantage, aptly summarised by Fr O'Laverty: "Unfortunately they adhered to the Celtic system of electing their chief from among the members of the dominant family [tanistry] … This elective principle in the choice of their chiefs led to bloodshed and ruinous contests on the death of each chief".

Such internecine rivalries persisted throughout the 15th century and tended to revolve around the main O'Neill castle in the centre of Belfast which often suffered damage in the process. By the time Conn O'Neill became chief the O'Neill hold on Belfast Castle had deminished and the family's seat had moved to the other proprietary castle of the Clandeboye O'Neills at Castlereagh.

Castlereagh

The castle at Castlereagh was built on the edge of an escarpment in the townland that acquired the same name, overlooking Belfast, as the Lord Chancellor of Ireland, Thomas Cusack, described it in 1553, "upon a plain in the midst of the woods of Dufferin" – a description which underpins its prominent, elevated view across the Lagan plain towards Belfast Lough. No vestige of the castle now remains, although the echoes of the voices of Conn's children at play can nowadays be heard on the site in the laughter and chatter of a children's day nursery which sits on the site at the top of Church Road.

The date of the construction of the castle of Castlereagh is uncertain but it is most probable that was constructed at some stage during the first half of the 16th century when the Clandeboye O'Neills faced increased internal rivalries and external pressures, which may in turn account for its commanding viewpoint. Although there is no unequivocal evidence to support the theory, it is possible that the establishment, fortunes and active life-time of the castle matched those of the nearby shrine at Knockcolumcille which, probably emerged in the first half of the 16th century and was abandoned in the first years of the subsequent century.

The first certain occupant was the second son of Niall Óg O'Neill (died 1537), Aodh (Hugh), who was chief of Upper Clandeboye from 1553 to 1555. Subsequently it passed to Conn, the last Gaelic O'Neill chieftain whose lordship of Clandeboye in the judgement of Conn's biographer in *The Dictionary of Irish Biography* "was characterised by his lack of judgement and dissolute ways, which squandered the advantages his father's judicious policies had snatched from the Elizabethan conquest" .

The only known artefact associated with the castle still preserved is the so-called stone coronation (or inauguration) chair apparently discovered amongst the ruins of the castle in 1755. This was shaped from whinstone (any hard, dark-coloured rock), 33" in height, with the seat carved at 15" from the ground. There is no unequivocal evidence of any such ceremony ever taking place and, if it had, it would probably have been conducted in the older O'Neill castle in Belfast. There is a strong probability that, if any such object existed, the English would at some stage have confiscated or destroyed it, and the likelihood is that the stone chair was simply a utilitarian domestic object carved from one of the quarries used to build the castle.

The size of the castle (approximately 100 ft x 100 ft) implies that it was built at a time when the O'Neill lords of Upper Clandeboye enjoyed a period of prosperity, and it probably proved impressive to contemporaries. In a map of 1602-1603 it is featured as a substantial square structure – one of the largest on the map – at the height of its service to the clan. Unfortunately the lack of any surviving evidence makes it impossible to determine the exterior aspect of the castle.

Although the considerable estates of Conn O'Neill featured significantly in the political turmoil of the late 16th century, and in the ambitions of Scottish carpet-baggers in the early 17th century, the castle quickly became redundant. The Hill family formally acquired it in December 1616. Nevertheless it clearly offered little charm to the interlopers and "it was abandoned as a major centre by the family in favour of Hillhall and Hillsborough".

It is alleged that an attempt was made in 1808 to prevent further erosion of the site by the erection of a surrounding wall, but that the mason accelerated the castle's destruction by using stone from the castle to build the wall – what one commentator described as "a truly Irish fate" – but this is probably an apocryphal tale, as such a wall already existed. By 1870 although the site was known, no structural vestige of the castle remained. In 1895 the local artist, J. W. Carey, made a partial drawing of the site, which revealed a few trees on a slight mound inside two low walls. With supreme political irony, the vacant site of the castle was eventually used in the 1930s to build an Orange Hall!

Conn O'Neill, the Last Gaelic Chieftain

The Gaelic control of Upper Clandeboye and the Great Ards (effectively north Down) during the last quarter of the 16th century is confusing. There must have been some suspicion amongst the O'Neill clan that this was something of a poisoned chalice.

Conn O'Neill had been in a strong position when he succeeded his father in early 1601. Chichester reported that Conn was a government pensioner (at 20 shillings per day, as his father had also been), and this added official approbation to his earlier election by the principle of tanistry. Initially Chichester had been inclined to divide the inheritance with one of Conn's cousins (Eoghan), but soon changed his mind and passed it on intact. As the historian George Benn suggested: "[Conn] lived at Castlereagh and, if he had been wise and prudent, might have continued to live there and transmitted his estates to his descendants".

The Loss of Upper Clandeboye (and the Great Ards)

The growing alienation and mutual disrespect between the native Irish and the various interlopers provided the background to the arrest and eventual territorial eradication of Conn O'Neill. It is a tale that has been elaborated from the time of its earliest narration, but the simpler reality is that the last Gaelic chieftain to grace (or disgrace) the Knock district was effectively the eponymous dupe of the events which followed – in other words, he was conned. The Scottish predators took full advantage of his naivety and lack of judgement.

It is related that towards the end of 1602 (or perhaps very early in 1603) Conn, a couple of his brothers and several others were engaged in an extended drinking session at Castlereagh; with supplies running short, he despatched a number of inebriated servants the two or three miles to Belfast to obtain more wine. They were assaulted by a handful of English soldiers and returned to the hill empty-handed. Conn was outraged at their ineptitude and sent them back into Belfast to fulfil their task. At some stage they had gathered weapons and, as a consequence of a renewed fight, some soldiers were injured and one died of his wounds. The Gaelic brawlers were chased back towards Conn's residence but, the commentator alleges, "The pursuit was not far because the soldiers feared a second assault from the hill of Castlereagh, where the said Conn, with his two brothers, friends and followers … stood, beholders of the chase".

As a result of this singular, trivial skirmish, the O'Neill dynasty of Upper Clandeboye disappeared within less than a generation and a whole new way of life – a new administration, new settlers and a more exploitative development of the locality – was imposed upon the Knockcolumcille district. The hybrid character which emerged and marginalized the native nucleus had become entrenched 200 years later.

Such a brawl as that over the wine, and even an occasional consequent death, was probably common-place in Belfast. An arrest for the death of the soldier could not have been unexpected, but the authorities elected to broadcast the belief that the events had been part of a treasonable plot on Conn's part against the Crown. The unpredictable loyalty of both Conn and his father during the previous four or five years made it easy for the authorities to adopt this interpretation, and the fact that it took a week to plan the arrest of Conn and his fellow-revellers adds to the suspicion of chicanery. Conn was quickly found guilty of levying war against the Queen and was held in custody in Carrickfergus Castle.

All historians and commentators have tended to take subsequent events at face value – that is, that a sympathetic Scot, Hugh Montgomery of Braidstane (anglicised to Broadstone) in Ayrshire, rescued Conn from his incarceration asking, in return, for half his lands. The evidence, however, suggests that he was the victim of long-term scheming on the part of the Scots and that he was totally unprepared for, and unequal to, the subterfuge and conspiracy which followed.

By late 1602 it was likely that Queen Elizabeth did not have long to live and it was known that her successor would be James VI of Scotland, who had been supplying rebels against the Crown in Ulster for some time. The Montgomery family was already engaged in commercial activity at Carrickfergus and would have been well-informed about developments such as the misfortune of Conn O'Neill. There can be no doubt that its skilful acquisition of Upper Clandeboye – even if it had ultimately to be shared reluctantly with the Hamiltons – bore all the hallmarks, if more subtle and less military, of the earlier planned interventions of John de Courcy (in 1177) and Sir Thomas Smith (in 1572).

A plan was hatched to stage-manage the escape of Conn from Carrickfergus. It is claimed that, following the accession of James as King of England on 24th March 1603, the Gaelic chieftain's conditions of incarceration were much relaxed: "It so came to pass that the said Conn had liberty to walk at his pleasure (in the day time) in the streets of Carrickfergus, and to entertain his friends and tenants in any victualling house within the town, having only a single sentinel to keep him in custody, and every night delivered him to the Marshal."

One of Montgomery's distant relations, who had traded regularly in the Co Antrim port, is said to have been induced to seduce the daughter of the Marshal and, after some months, was able to utilise the relationship to arrange the release Conn from his cell and take him to Scotland. A future Presbyterian minister of Donaghadee, Rev Andrew Stewart (1645-1671), also later wrote that Conn's second wife, Eilis Ni Neill, colluded with the Montgomery family to facilitate his escape by smuggling ropes into her husband in two large hollowed-out cheeses. Whilst this elaboration adds a frisson to the tale, it is both an improbable and superfluous confection if Conn's cell door were simply being left unlocked. Indeed, such a subterfuge was more likely to draw attention to the plot, as cheese appears to have been a rarity in the Irish diet at that time.

(The later Sir) Hugh Montgomery, who had engineered the whole enterprise, welcomed the Ulster chieftain, congratulated him on "his happy escape" and subsidised his interim expenses. Conn "was kindly entertained and treated with a due deference to his birth and quality". Montgomery informed the Clandeboye chieftain that he was in a position at court to "procure his pardon for all his and [his followers'] crimes and transgressions against the law ... and [he] should get the inquest to be vacated [i.e abandoned]". The hospitality was, however, motivated by pure self-interest and, in return for his supposedly generous intercession at court (which appears to cost him £1000), Montgomery required Conn to sign over to him half of the extensive Upper Clandeboye. Timothy McCall has also commented that "the least explicable element in this episode is the initial agreement between Montgomery and Conn O'Neill. Why exactly Conn felt in need of such a pardon is never made clear".

McCall's interpretation was that the Gaelic chieftain had his own agenda, and that "Conn was a willing partner in this arrangement because he stood to gain security for the lands which he wanted in Castlereagh". McCall argued that Conn had not been accorded legal possession of Castlereagh and the Great Ards – they were held purely on the designation by tanistry. He was prepared to sacrifice a substantial amount of his Gaelic inheritance to the Scots in order to gain undisputed title to the heartland of Castlereagh: "He gave Hamilton and Montgomery what was not his, to gain what he claimed to be his". It is, however, doubtful that Conn O'Neill ever had such intellectual political sophistication and, if he did, it was a very high risk strategy which could have resulted in the loss of everything.

The victors write history. Just as, in retrospect, the Norman chroniclers justified William of Normandy's claim to England by depicting on the Tapestry Harold's oath at Bayeux, Hugh Montgomery concealed his contrived plot to acquire Irish lands with a concocted invention of Conn's gratitude and consent.

In the event he had to divide his territories three ways, as outlined in an indenture of 30th April 1605. James Hamilton, originally an academic, had more influence at court than Montgomery, and successfully petitioned for a claim. The indenture was issued "in consideration of the King's pardon to Conn O'Neill, and the grant of his lands to Hamilton, and of the expenses of Montgomery and Hamilton in procuring that pardon and grant", and the fact that the two Scotsmen had maintained Conn and his followers in England from August 1604.

The Return of Conn O'Neill

Conn was fortunate to retain Castlereagh as the heartland of his portion, but he had to suffer the indignity of having English and Scottish settlers imposed upon a third of his remaining estate, even if they were "paying him reasonable rents, to be agreed on". Shortly after the initial arrangement, Conn returned to Scotland and appears to have finally reached Castlereagh via Dublin in July 1605, having been absent from the locality for at least two and a half years. The compiler of the Montgomery Manuscripts, William Montgomery, asserts that "Conn then returned home in triumph over his enemies … and was met by his friends, tenants and followers"; however, as a consequence of the loss of much of his territory and his lengthy absence, his arrival probably proved to be much more subdued.

On 6th November 1605, on the day on which torture was being applied to some of those engaged in the previous day's failed Gunpowder Plot, Conn was suffering a more subtle form of pain – having to accept the indenture of James Hamilton for what had been his own inheritance. One commentator has argued that his new holdings showed that "Conn O'Neill was still to be a person of consequence"; he was confirmed in 60 townlands which "begin on the left bank of the Lagan at Lambeg, then proceed along the right bank as far as Holywood, and from that base project south-easterly into Co Down at least eight miles".

There may have been some consolation in the fact that the lands around his castle remained the heartland of his reduced territory, and included Holywood, Ballyhanwood, Lisnabreeny, Ballymacarrett, Breda, Ballymaconaghy, Ballynafeigh, Ballyrushboy, Galwally, Cregagh, Castlereagh and Knockcolumcille. He was permitted to hold a weekly market at Holywood and Castlereagh with the related courts, such as those of pie-powder, but these would have generated a very small income.

Such occasions, however, encapsulated Conn's difficulties – in addition to the fact that his personal holding had greatly contracted, the nature of it had also changed. He was forced to adopt alien methods of administration and accounting. Within four or five years of his return to Castlereagh he had sold or leased estate in addition to his lands beyond the immediate vicinity of present-day Knock – in Ballymechan, Ballymacarrett, Ballynafeigh, Ballymaconaghy, Ballyrushboy, Galwally and Breda. There are occasional hints of an emotional bond to his patrimony when, within grants, he excepted the woods of his Castlereagh demesne and the right of patronage to the church of Knockcolumcille; in the majority of instances, however, he also readily sacrificed attached grazing, mining and timber rights. The latter reflects the amount of building which was being undertaken to accommodate the influx of settlers, as at Holywood under Hamilton in addition to the growth of Belfast.

The symbolic end of the O'Neill era came on 23 May 1618 when, whilst paying technical acknowledgement to Conn, both Hamilton and Montgomery issued detailed reciprocal deeds relating to the area (and beyond). The final insult, calculated or otherwise, may well have been the fact that "Delivery and seisin were made in the fields of Knockcolumcille in the territory of Castlereagh". Even the essence of Conn's historical association with the district – the dynastic nomenclature: Clann Aodha Buidhe (Clandeboye) – was transferred four years later when, on 4 March 1622, Sir James Hamilton was created Viscount Clandeboye. Times had irreversibly changed and, for all the favour and prominence Conn's elder son, Daniel O'Neill, was to enjoy at the English court, his later efforts to recover his family's inheritance proved unsuccessful.

Conn died in 1619, it is said (without any real proof) at Holywood. It is claimed that he was buried in the churchyard at Ballymaghan (technically a possession of the Abbey of Bangor), where the present-day Motelands joins the Old Holywood Road. Why this place was chosen is impossible to determine, but it may not have been without significance that Lewis's *Topographical Dictionary* indicates that the alternative name for Ballymaghan was Columcille. Additionally, whilst all the other churches in the locality are still listed in 1622 as 'ruins' after half a century of warfare, there appears to have been no surviving church at Ballymaghan, which at least implied a dignified final resting-place for an erstwhile Gaelic chieftain. Indeed, the location appears to have been of sufficient stature to play host to an official Inquisition 'near Ballymaghan' on 5 November 1625.

THE SCOTTISH SETTLEMENT

The Scots were attracted to settle in what is now the Castlereagh or wider Knock district by the patent opportunities which the region offered. Contemporary observers described Great Ards (north Down) as "champion and fertile land". There was an acknowledgement that in South Clandeboye as a whole there existed "an extent of desolation seldom produced even by the dire agencies of war", and when the first settlers arrived in the Newtownards and Greyabbey area in May 1606 they were probably faced by similar challenging circumstances which were soon afterwards to greet the Pilgrim Fathers. Nevertheless, to those of an adventurous and industrious pioneer disposition, the abundant locality offered a ready supply of timber, free stone and slate (particularly greywacke slate used in roofing), and a fallow terrain to cultivate. There was a range of land: when James Hamilton added the barony of Dufferin to his portfolio in 1610 it was said that he acquired 15000 acres of arable land, 1000 acres of pasture, 10000 acres of woodland and 2000 acres of heath and moor. One of the principal inspirations amongst the emigrants was Montgomery's wife, Elizabeth, who encouraged the establishment of orchards and gardens, the building of watermills – a novelty in Ulster – and the development of linen and woollen manufacturing.

To a degree, the absence of any serious resistance to the settlement in the area was the consequence of the demise of the O'Neill influence in the region, and was reflected during the next quarter of a century in the growth of Belfast, which was then perceived less as a strategic and military necessity and more as a trading centre. Close links between Knock and Belfast – whose growth was more closely associated with the north of Belfast Lough and along the Lagan valley – did not develop for the best part of another century; the bridge across the Lagan to Ballymacarrett was not constructed until 1680, and a road to Newtownards was not built until 1757.

At the time of the early settlement the woods were still infested with uncouth woodkerne and large numbers of unemployed and aimless native Irish soldiers. Despite this, the emigrants who arrived in Co. Down appear to have experienced much less hostility than those who established the plantation of Ulster more to the west. Rev Andrew Stewart of Donaghadee was not complimentary about the character of the some of the Scottish settlers, describing them as "scum" who left Scotland for dubious reasons, but these were probably outnumbered by those who arrived with a laudable pioneer attitude.

The greatest cross-Channel exodus occurred during the first eight years. By 1614 estimates place the number of Scottish males in Co Down at between 2000 and 3000 (about 100 of whom were named Hamilton or Montgomery). The early 17th century was to witness the erosion of the Gaelic presence and influence in the Knock district as, as Gillespie expressed it, "the triumph of a new social and economic order". The lack of decisive leadership by Conn O'Neill in the first score of years set the pattern. This was compounded the fact that he had either sacrificed or sold most of his estate, and that the new landlords were prohibited from accepting native Irish tenants.

By the time of Conn's death in 1619 there were precious few markers of the Gaelic past remaining. Around 1643 the peripatetic Franciscan, Edmund MacCana, commented on the desolation of the ancient Celtic monasteries: "of these not even the ruins remain, for a colony of Scots who settled there employed the stones of them for building houses for themselves". It is more likely that this practice was pursued more for convenience and practicality rather than in the pursuit of deliberate obliteration implied in the friar's coda: "so great is the passion of heretics for demolishing sacred objects".

Presbyterians

By the mid-17th century the Scottish Presbyterian presence was more evident with churches – always a sign of an established and growing population – having been built at Dundonald, Holywood, Knock and Breda, as well as in the larger townships. The two latter meeting houses were ultimately amalgamated in 1720 in the Castlereagh Hills, close to the ruins of Conn's erstwhile residence

– which may well have been used as a quarry for the church's construction.

This is not the forum to discuss the increasing tensions between the Episcopal authorities and the expanding Presbyterian Church. The hostility between the two denominations was to endure in the area into the early 19th century. The Castlereagh Hills were to provide a singular illustration. In 1786 Robert Leathem built Leathem Cottage – also reputed to be a beneficiary of the adjacent rubble from Conn O'Neill's derelict castle – at the end of Church Road, one hundred yards beyond the site of the Presbyterian Church. This was the era of the Volunteers and the United Irishmen and Leathem was alleged to be a government agent or spy, who rather gave the lie to the judgement of Rev. William Rogers (who was called to Castlereagh in 1871) that "the outstanding characteristic of Castlereagh people from generation to generation … [is that they] are truly kind-hearted and possess the love that never fails". Leathem accused his neighbour, Rev. Alexander Henry, the minister at the Presbyterian Church (1774 to 1806) of uttering seditious words – although the latter was to be "honourably acquitted" of the charge. As Leathem lived on until November 1813, he may not have proved popular with his Presbyterian neighbours.

It may be fair to conclude that the quality of the 17th century Presbyterian clergy was higher than that of the Episcopal Church, primarily because it had to struggle to assert its case against the entrenched blasé authoritarianism of the latter, but one historian of Co. Down concluded that neither denomination won the struggle for predominance, and during the second half of the 17th century both proved equally intolerant.

The religious and spiritual struggle faced by the Scots was matched by the temporal and material difficulties. Although they proved more adept at exploiting the commercial possibilities of South Clandeboye, this was not a period of unremitting economic success. Capital investment proved thin, and there were to be a series of harvest failures in the late 1630s. The situation was exacerbated by the turbulent 1640s, when Gaelic frustrations resulted in one last act of defiance. In late October 1641 the native Irish in parts of Ulster made one final attempt to remove their oppressors. The subsequent months of conflict cultivated some horrific tales, including the death of 954 people in one morning in Co. Antrim, and of 80 men, women and children forced on to the ice to drown in Lough Neagh.

Castlereagh appears to have escaped the worst of this unedifying drama, although there were occasional incidents in the locality. On 17th December 1641 a Scottish officer, Hugh Montgomery, reported from Comber that "rebels burn and kill every other night within a mile, two or three unto us, neither can we help it". The worst incident occurred near Craigavad with "the atrocious massacre of 73 persons" at the end of January 1642 (possibly in the townland of Ballydavey) which "seems to have completely cleared the parish of the old Irish race". The latter event may have been prompted by the arrival, on the other side of the Lough, of 2500 Scottish troops in the town and castle of Carrickfergus. This force took control of Belfast in May 1644 – and it was after this that the Presbyterians began to show their confidence by creating their Congregations and Sessions.

Perhaps the most bizarre indication that life in the region was not quite so fraught as elsewhere in Ulster (and Ireland) was the itinerary of the friar Edmund MacCana, who is alleged to have made his tour of the area – encompassing Bangor, Comber, Newtownards, Movilla, Holywood and Knockcolumcille, and through Belfast as far as Whiteabbey and Carrickfergus – around the year 1643 or 1644. Bearing in mind the recent events in Holywood and on the other side of Belfast Lough it was a courageous, if not foolhardy, venture by one of his religious persuasion.

Gaelic landowners and aristocracy appear to have effectively vanished after this uprising. Nevertheless the immediate heirs and successors of both Hamilton and Montgomery appear to have been devoid of the talent and commitment of their predecessors and this, plus natural circumstances, made it difficult for the Scottish landholders to prosper as they would have desired. Jonathan Bardon states that "the province was in a wretched economic condition on the accession of Charles II [1660]", and the signs are that there was a surprising degree of poverty in some local communities at the opening of the 18th century.

Knock In The Modern Era

The Knock area experienced gradual growth and settlement for a century and a half, then accelerated. An interconnecting road network emerged during the first half of the 18th century. A map of 1714 displays the road from Lisburn via Hillhall and Cairnshill to Castlereagh, and continuing to Bangor via Ballymaghan and Cultra. Another route diverts from the Castlereagh Hills via Gransha to Comber. A quarter of a century later another map indicates that a road from the latter passed through Dundonald to meet the route which ran from the Long Bridge via Beersbridge to Newtownards – although at that stage it traversed the hill behind the current Stormont location. A more direct route was established early in the second half of the century, following that of the present-day to Dundonald, taking the old route (via Dundonald Mill) to Newtownards. Another thoroughfare, which effectively follows the current Belmont Road, existed at least as early as 1767, but it has to be conceded that the standard of these roads left much to be desired well into the 19th century.

Rural Ambience

The area long retained its rural ambience, which made it popular with the commercial and industrial classes of Belfast who wished to escape the noise, grime and crowding of their business environment. The estates of the Londonderry family in the Knockbreda area (in such townlands as Lisnabreeny and Ballmaconaghy) were assessed for their value according to the number of livestock or the size of the crops. The fact that farming was a primary livelihood at this time in the Knockbreda parish is reflected in the fact that on 22 October 1814 the farmers formed an association which successfully challenged the imposition of tolls over the Long Bridge and into the Belfast markets. At the eastern boundary of the locality, at Richmond Lodge, Francis Turnly (who had returned from China in 1801 with a reputed fortune in excess of £60,000) even intensified the scene; he contacted the lessor, David McCance, to negotiate a concession against his rent because, in the four years to 1809, he had registered the planting of 9810 "forest trees, evergreen and flowering shrubs, fruit trees, fruit bushes, etc".

The locality came to be dotted with an increasing number of mansions and villas. Even before the end of the 18th century, Holywood played host to a number of substantial residences: Holywood House (1740), Ballymenoch (1780, later home to businessman Cunningham Greg), Clifton House and Craigavad House (both c.1783), and Rockport and Richmond Lodge (both c.1800) established by John and Francis Turnly. Close to the present-day Knock junction, Thornhill (then known as Thornyhill) and Tullycarnet appear on a map of 1783 – and may precede that date by a few years – and Lewis's *Topographical Dictionary* reports the neighbouring properties of Summerfield, Rosepark and Stormont close to Dundonald by the late 1830s.

During his travels in the early 1740s, Walter Harris noted the adjacent property at Castle Hill, in addition to Dunlady (at

Dundonald) and, more distantly, Orangefield, a close neighbour of the Raineys at Greenville, which also dated to the mid-18th century. One of the principal villas in the locality was Belmont (on the estate which now hosts Campbell College) dating back to the 1750s; its neighbour – Cabin Hill – was built in 1785 by Martha McTier and her husband, Sam.

The domestic economy proved important and enduring to such estates. In 1801 Martha enthused about "the dairy, garden and meadow in rich abundance" at Cabin Hill, yet even three quarters of a century later when the contents of a home in Palmerston Terrace in Sydenham were auctioned (in February 1875), in addition to the manifold domestic possessions, the lots included "a first class milch cow … farm cart and harness, contents of a greenhouse … [and] potatoes, hay and manure". It remained a useful selling point in the Belmont locality well into the second half of the 19th century that even smaller properties could boast that "the land is well drained, fenced and nicely planted with forest trees of ten years' growth". In 1875 the detached villa named Herbertville (close to the current King's Road) offered a "vinery, greenhouse and tastefully laid-out garden", and when Mrs Ferris auctioned her residence in Sydenham Park in Strandtown on 15 January 1875 she promoted her "good productive garden, and land of approximately one acre, well-enclosed and neatly planted". At that time all the major residences in that area employed their own gardeners, including Thomas Spence at Cabin Hill, George Ramsay at the Moat House and William McCracken at Belmont.

Residential Expansion

Into the first third of the 19th century the numbers of inhabitants did not rise dramatically. The *Ordnance Survey Memoirs* recorded that in the early 1830s there were marginally over 3000 people living in the area between Holywood (which boasted 1300 of that number) and Ballyhackamore (with just over 600). These mansions and villas, however, engaged a wide range of employees, both domestic and managerial. Even an *ad hoc* parochial list drawn up in 1873 by the minister at Knockbreda indicates that nearby Belvoir House employed gardeners, labourers, ploughmen, woodsmen, grooms, dairymaids, gatekeepers and others. The school registers at Belmont National School, which opened in 1862, reveal that the large local residences also employed coachmen, butlers and valets, kitchen staff, and a range of workers from unskilled labourers to the more professional land stewards.

Such schools were an irrefutable sign of the growth of a settled population. The *Ordnance Survey Memoirs* show that many of the townlands and townships in the wider Knock area boasted their own schools by the early 19th century. There were five located in Holywood alone. In 1820 on the eastern edge of Holywood, at the gates of their home, Rockport (in the townland of Ballyrobert), the wife of John Turnly founded a school which still exists in the guise of Glencraig. From 1818 John Turnly himself patronised a school at the other side of the town in Knocknagoney, which catered for 90 pupils. In 1906 Rockport itself was transformed into a prep school which still functions in a broader capacity.

The population expansion of the locality and its educational needs was perhaps most noticeably articulated by the establishment in 1862 of Belmont National School, originally attached to the newly-founded Presbyterian Church, although relocated on 4 August 1890 on the Belmont Road. The earliest registers demonstrate that the parents of the pupils came from a wide range of social backgrounds which encompassed both traditional rural occupations and those of a more urban nature. Many varied occupations, trades and professions were represented including customs official, postmaster, constable, stationmaster, auctioneer, photographer, jeweller, watchmaker, nurseryman, missionary, sea captain, tea trader and bookseller. The more central focus of Belmont and Knock is indicated by the fact that, in addition to these two districts, the National School's pupils were attracted from as wide a field as Gilnahirk, Dundonald, Tullycarnet, Ballymiscaw, Ballymisert, Ballycloughan, Strandtown, Sydenham, Ballyhackamore and Bloomfield, and even as distantly as Mountpottinger and Ballymacarrett.

During the 19th century the latter district, despite its narrow geographical proportions, was to absorb a population which exceeded that of many Irish towns and cities. In 1837 First Ballymacarrett Presbyterian Church was carved out of the extensive congregation of Castlereagh created in 1720 which, with its tall distinctive cupola, had only just become one of the more prominent, identifiable sentinels in the district. The new church was opened in 1835 at the top of Church Road, just as the splinter with Ballymacarrett was approved.

Denomination and Devotion

Piety and devotion partnered unlikely and ironic bedfellows and heralded changing times in the area. Rev Hugh Wilson, the first Presbyterian minister (then in charge of the two parishes of Knock and Breda), had been deprived of his charge in 1661 by Bishop Jeremy Taylor, and two years later suffered the same fate as Conn O'Neill – who had lived only one hundred yards from the site of the future church – of being imprisoned in Carrickfergus Castle. The rancorous contretemps at the close of the 18th century between Robert Leathem and Rev Alexander Henry reflected the malice which could result from the admixture of religion and politics.

Yet the world had clearly mellowed a third of a century later; those who turned out at the inaugural service in the new church, to listen to Rev Henry Haslett expound upon the text *You are Peter, the rock, and upon this rock I will build my church* (Matthew XVI, 18), included a number of prominent Episcopalians such as Sir Robert Bateson (originally of Orangefield, but by then living at Belvoir Park).

It became common-place during the 19th century – as at the foundation of the three churches at Knock – that members of all denominations encouraged and assisted in the establishment of new places of worship. One other Episcopalian member of the congregation at Castlereagh on that Sunday, 16 August 1835, may well have indulged a knowing smile as he passed the site of Conn O'Neill's ruined castle on his way to the service. The fourth son of the 2nd Marquess of Donegall bore the same name as his ancestor who had besieged that very spot almost exactly 234 years previously: Sir Arthur Chichester!

One of Haslett's successors, Rev William Rogers, was to intimate in the last quarter of the century that the pace of life in the hills was gentler than in the expanding metropolis below: "Time", he asserted, "was not measured by city clocks in Castlereagh". Whatever the truth of this perspective, the reality was that Presbyterians placed great emphasis upon the work ethic; one subscribed to the view that "Young people soon saw that life was a serious business, and that there was little room in it for play or amusement; that hard work, and prayer and worship were the only fit occupations of rational people". The families of both Haslett and Rogers were to become involved in commercial activity. One of Haslett's sons became a druggist and chemist, as well as penultimate Mayor of Belfast, and another founded a substantial grocery empire; Rogers's younger brother became engaged in the flax trade in Banbridge, which included business ventures in Belgium.

The local Church of Ireland adopted a more liberated ethos, perhaps most evidently cultivated by the rector of Knockbreda Parish Church, Rev John Kinahan (1824-1866), who took time off from his pastoral cares to father sixteen children (eight sons and eight daughters)! In the mid-17th century Knock and Breda had been united with Dundonald, all served by a single rector from 1634 to 1758. The parishioners of all three districts seemed content for the best part of a century to worship in the centrally-located, but probably increasingly derelict church of the O'Neill foundation on the hill of Knock(columcille). They, however, appear to have exhibited the same predilection for making tax-collecting difficult, which Conn O'Neill had encountered a century earlier. The rector of Knockbreda and (as Dundonald was then known) Kirkdonnell from 1713 to 1729 was Rev James Hamilton, who was resident – for part of that time at least – at Castle Hill (close to the current Stormont). He engaged an agent named H Neill to collect the tithes owed to him, and it is not without irony that he experienced the same indifference and problems which had faced his Gaelic namesake.

Neill was treated with total contempt. On 7 January 1720 he reported that he had arranged for "the parishioners of Knock and Breda to meet me last Thursday at Castlereagh, where I stayed the length of the day". In retrospect, he may have felt that selecting the last day of the year (31 December 1719) had not proved the wisest choice, for he stayed until late in the afternoon but had to report that "Not three of them came near me"! Nettled, he continued: "I see no other way of handling these unreasonable people than to let them be till about Candlemas [2 February], and then see everyone that did not pay part for the whole".

Nearly three years later he still manifested little aptitude as a tithe-gatherer. On 17 November 1722 Neill reported from Castlereagh that the previous day's storm had "hindered the parishioners to meet me at Belfast" – only four had turned up! He promised that "I shall be at Belfast and here [Castlereagh] in a fortnight's time and frequent the parish once a fortnight till I finish with them". He concluded rather plaintively and unconvincingly that "Though

I owe you a great deal of money, please God I shall pay you honestly".

It may have been such persistent problems that encouraged, at the start of 1724, "the bargain and sale … to Rt Hon Thomas Knox of Dungannon of certain tithes arising from the lands of Ballymaghan and Strandtown (alias Ballymisert) and rectorial tithes of Knock (alias Knockcolumcille) in the manor Holywood, situate and lying in the Barony of Castlereagh". The payment of £420 16s 2d by Thomas Knox represents the beginning of the latter family's interest in the Knock district which they were ultimately to sell to Thomas McClure.

The reluctance to pay tithes is an echo of the fact that not everyone in the district was a devout worshipper. When William Rainey of Greenville died on 12 June 1803 he was buried at the family mausoleum that graces Knockbreda graveyard, yet – as his friend and near neighbour, Martha McTier, revealed – he was "supposed to be an unbeliever … [and] never went to any place of worship". Seventy years later, the minister at Knockbreda, Rev Henry Stewart, ruefully noted that John McKeown, the local innkeeper, was "seldom at church" and William Parker, the butcher, "never comes to church".

The proliferation of churches was not only indicative of burgeoning population but also of an emerging sense of local identity. The union of Dundonald, Knock and Breda had been determined in 1657, but in the 1730s the parishioners of the latter decided to accept the offer of Anne, Dowager Viscountess Midleton, to build a new church "at her own expense in a more convenient place" (Knockbreda), which was ready for worship on 7 August 1737. Lady Ikerrin (of the Hamilton dynasty from Bangor), who lived at Castle Hill in the parish of Dundonald, was unenthusiastic about travelling the greater distance for Sunday worship, and appealed – unsuccessfully – to the Bishop. By 1758 Dundonald had its own rector, although it waited until 1771 to provide him with church, described as "a small edifice".

Just over a century later Knock could boast the inauguration of three denominational churches within a quarter of a mile of one another. The first to open was the Methodist church in 1870, followed two years later by the Presbyterians. The latter, as had been the case at Ballymacarrett, was the offspring of the Castlereagh congregation and, by coincidence, the minister of the latter, William Rogers, will have ridden past the construction site at Knock each Sunday on his way to Church Road between 1871 and 1874, as he lived with his aunt on the Holywood Road in Strandtown until his own manse was completed that year. The first full service at Knock – which was known until 1921 as Dundela – was on 27 January 1876.

At this time, riding was still remarkably common-place. Like Rogers, his fellow Presbyterian, the second minister at Knock (from December 1889), Rev James Hunter, used to visit his parishioners on horseback and, as so many of the early congregation at the adjacent Methodist church rode to services, two years after its foundation it was obliged to add stabling.

To that extent little had changed since Columcille had, arguably, ridden through the region over 1300 years previously on his way to Movilla, and when the Church of Ireland consecrated its new foundation close by on 13 June 1896, it was named in his honour: St Columba's. Bearing in mind that Columba's missionary travels appear ultimately to have begun as a result of the offence he caused Finnian, it was not inappropriate that, when the parish began to grow numerically in the Cregagh area (between Knockbreda and Knock) in the late 1920s and early 1930s, they named the new foundation after the founder of Movilla.

Thomas McClure

Knock and its adjacent districts of Sydenham, Strandtown and Belmont owed much of their character and development to the amiable, visionary and ecumenical (later Sir) Thomas McClure (1806-1893), who followed in the Presbyterian, mercantile footsteps of his ancestors.

Thomas was born on 4 March 1806, the second son of William McClure, a prosperous Belfast merchant – who lived in Donegall Place when it was still residential – "whose ships", it was claimed, "sailed to all parts of the world". *The Northern Whig* recorded that Messrs Wm McClure & Son were "general merchants, but shortly afterwards became connected with the shipping trade; and for a time grain and tea received their special attention". Thomas joined his father's business at 16 Corporation Street, also becoming a tobacco manufacturer and setting up business with his cousins (Charles and William Laird Finlay) as yarn and linen merchants. One, somewhat sycophantic, assessment of McClure in 1869 projected him as "one of the mercantile fathers of modern Belfast ... As a commercial gentleman we unhesitatingly place him second to no merchant in Belfast", but there can be little doubt that his business acumen brought him considerable wealth, and his purchase of extensive and expensive real estate in East Belfast in the late 1850s would suggest that he proved to be a very able businessman and entrepreneur.

On 1 October 1856 the Commissioners of the Encumbered Estates in Ireland agreed to the sale to McClure of lands belonging to Thomas Knox, second Earl of Ranfurly, and to the latter's younger son (and seventh child), Rt Hon William Stuart Knox, and (by an earlier agreement with the Knox family dating back to 1790) to Daniel McLornan, who then resided at Knock House in the area (and who died on 13 June 1868). The Rent Books of Sir Thomas McClure and the papers of his estate indicate that, by July 1857, he had paid £13,000 for the Knock properties of the Ranfurly estate and £28,500 for those in Strandtown. His additional purchase – for the sum of £31,371 – of the Knock properties of one John Dawson was registered in March 1858. Consequently McClure now owned a wide swathe of real estate which effectively stretched from the Belmont and Knock locality down to the shore of Belfast Lough. Since the 1750s there had been a residence on the seventy-acre Belmont estate which McClure also purchased before 1858 from the fourth Viscount Bangor. He resided there (accompanied by his sister, Eliza, who died in December 1878) until it was sold in late 1890 to the Trustees of the will of Henry James Campbell for the creation of Campbell College.

McClure's acquisition of the Ranfurly estates – which encompassed much of the Strandtown, Sydenham, Belmont and Knock districts – was a deliberate and calculated effort to develop the area. One source noted that within a decade "the whole neighbourhood is fast becoming one of the most marked for elegant and permanent improvements in the immediate vicinity of the Great Linen Metropolis". In his *History of the County of Down*, Alexander Knox recorded that: "A considerable proportion of the district, studded with handsome villas, is now the property of Sir Thomas McClure who, by forming convenient roads, fences and plantations, and granting long building leases, has given a great impetus to improvements in the district". By 1875, McClure was advertising in the local press, offering what he described as 'most eligible building lots' as villa sites in the neighbourhood of Belmont, Newtownards Road and Knock.

McClure inherited the Ranfurly leases with his tenants, such as that for Redburn with John Dunville (dated 31 January 1848) and with John Hutchinson Garner for Garnerville (dated 28 December 1854). The new proprietor was, however, not solely interested in the financial benefits of leasing, but primarily in the residential development of the locality and he encouraged this by offering leases for 10,000 years. When buildings such as the Moat House, on the Old Holywood Road adjacent to Garnerville, already existed, the renewal of the lease (in this case, on 20 August 1863 with Thomas Valentine) required the lessor to maintain the edifice. In other instances he imposed an obligation to build. On 31 March 1873 he leased nine acres for 10,000 years to William Ewart junior on condition that, by 1 November 1874, Ewart had built at his own expense "the said demised premises and completely furnish fit for habitation and use as a Villa residence, messuage or dwelling house with proper outhouses". This probably related to the development of Glenmachan House, but there had also been an earlier arrangement (on 26 April 1865) with Ewart for eighteen acres of land known as Schomberg Park on which he was obliged to build, before 1 May 1867, premises which were fit for habitation and use for at least twenty years as "a villa residence".

On 7 September 1876, on the boundary between the townlands of Ballycloughan and Ballymaghan, William Robertson leased 31 acres on condition that he build a house – which became Netherleigh – by 1 May 1879. The arrangement in 1884 with Charles William Barnett of Thornhill (which had already been occupied since the late 18th century) was that the latter should also keep in good repair the associated paths and roads. Similarly, when on 12 May 1864 Henry Smith leased eighteen acres on the Old Holywood Road (between the Moat House and what is now the Cairnburn Road) both the lessee and McClure agreed to maintain the road and to repair the embankment "until it becomes a county road", and to maintain the drains and water pipes.

Although McClure encouraged his tenants to develop the economic opportunities of their own estates, he did not surrender his traditional rights and privileges as a landowner. His lease of 10 July 1868 (which continued an earlier agreement of March 1828) to the widow Maria Freeman in the townland of Knock required herself, her heirs, executors and under-tenants:

> *[to grind] all their corn, malt or grain that shall be expended upon the said premises or that shall be by them ground for sale at such Mill or Mills within the manor aforesaid as the said Thomas McClure ... shall from time to time under their hand or hands in writing direct and appoint not being more than 10 miles distant from the said granted premises, and paying the accustomed mulcture or grist for grinding the same or, on failure thereof, yielding and paying to the said Thomas McClure ... the sum of 10 shillings sterling for every barrel of grain ground at any other Mill ...*

The neighbours of Maria Freeman were the Gelston family (whose land was situated at what is now the junction of Shandon Park and the Knock dual carriageway). The original agreement between William Gelston and the Hon Thomas Knox dated back to 1794. This lease was renewed between Thomas McClure and John Gelston, designated as a farmer, on 21 June 1861 and the latter agreed that he should grind all his corn and grain at "McClure's Mill at 10 shillings per barrel", although the specific location was actually left blank on the lease. Additionally, whilst repair would be made to any damage to the surface of disturbed soil, McClure and his agents were allowed free access to his tenants' estates "to search for natural resources – coals, manure, marble, limestone, etc, etc", and he retained access for the watering of cattle and flax, and "free passage for horses and carriages to mosses and bogs, and also to Church, Mill, kiln and market" (although much of this legal vocabulary derives from the original 17th century grants).

Thomas McClure was raised in the Presbyterian tradition. He was an Elder at the Fisherwick Place congregation before assuming the same status at Belmont, and he was active on a number of the Committees of the General Assembly of the Presbyterian Church in Ireland. One of his wills, dated 2 February 1880, left half of his wealth to the Presbyterian Church, and was responsible for the creation of a number of Presbyterian churches in the locality. In 1870 a Sunday School met in McClure's Knock Mill at the junction of the Knock and Cheryvalley Roads. Subsequently, the congregation sought a new church – Knock Presbyterian (although between 1875 and 1921 it was known as Dundela) – for which the recently knighted Sir Thomas laid the foundation stone on 9 November 1875.

McClure was also the effective founder of Belmont Presbyterian Church. The official indenture of the lease between the merchant and Trustees of the congregation (which included McClure's cousin, and trustee of his own will, William Laird Finlay) was made as late as 10 August 1868, but in 1860 he had consented to the original application for two acres for 10,000 years at the peppercorn rent of 10 shillings per annum for the site of a House of Worship, school house, manse and porter's lodge – for the building of which he also donated £1600. The church held its first service on 26 June 1862, and was graced a bell presented by his sister, Eliza.

His older brother, William, was minister to the congregation of First Derry Church for 49 years, and served as Moderator of the General Synod in 1834-1835 and Moderator of the General Assembly in 1847-1848. As part of his Moderator's address on 4 July 1848 to the General Assembly, William spoke of the realities of "the degradation of vast multitudes in the metropolis of these kingdoms", and drew attention to illiteracy, the neglect of spiritual welfare, deserted children and homes of "wretchedness and profligacy".

These were social issues of which his merchant brother must have become increasingly cognisant from the late 1850s as he travelled between Corporation Street and Belmont, through the expanding mass of Ballymacarrett which harboured a population as large as most Irish towns and cities. Thomas McClure was clearly a man with a social conscience; in the longer version of his will he urged his beneficiaries to be mindful that "wealth and competence should always be enjoyed within moderate bounds and limits, and that 'unto whomsoever much is given of him shall much be required' at that last great day when we shall all stand before the Judgement seat and render unto the Almighty an account of our Stewardship". His philanthropy and charitable acts were unostentatious and, significantly, inclusive. Such ecumenism was evident to one contemporary who claimed that: "His popularity, however, is by no means limited by Presbyterian restrictions ... Though Mr McClure is a decided Presbyterian, no man can be more esteemed among all sections of the community. He deems it unnecessary to support his own views at the expense of the honesty or Christian sincerity of others".

His tolerant and receptive manner was evident in his rather fraught and inconspicuous political career between 1868 and 1885. In 1868, with Catholic support, he became the last Liberal candidate elected to a Belfast parliamentary seat and, in 1874, he was elected for a Co Londonderry seat. He lacked charisma but it was said of him that "He is emphatically a good, honest, sincere man … a plain, blunt, straightforward, friendly man". Although he was never a prominent Member of Parliament, he represented and spoke on behalf of all sections of the community and advocated political and social reform. He was awarded a baronetcy in March 1874.

On 18 October 1877, at the age of 71, Sir Thomas consolidated the historic links between the east coast of Ulster and Scotland by unexpectedly marrying a 35-year-old Scot, Ellison Thorburn Macfie (at Dreghorn Castle near Edinburgh). Following the sale of Belmont estate to the Trustees of Campbell College in 1890, he and his wife moved in July to Edinburgh, where he died on 19 January 1893. He made five wills between February 1885 and August 1891 which inevitably made provision for his newly-acquired wife, but much of his estate was left to the Presbyterian Church.

More significantly, his final codicil manifested the landowner's continuing concern for the development of the locality. He instructed his Trustees to raise £1200 "out of the dividends, interest and income thereof, to pay all such sums of money, wages, salaries and expenses as may be necessary for keeping in repair, renewing, restoring and preserving the Embankment or sea wall surrounding part of my lands at Strandtown and which separates my said lands from the tidal river called Connswater, or any part of the sluice gates, towers and caretaker's residence, valves and machinery now used or to be hereinafter used in connection therewith".

Wider Boundaries

Although he was to become despondent at their lack of profitability, McClure was also – from a commercial perspective – a great advocate of the railways, and the Belfast, Holywood & Bangor Railway through Sydenham and Holywood, and the Belfast & County Down Railway stations at Knock (opened 1850) and Bloomfield (opened 1879), provided easier access to Belfast for the industrial and professional classes.

They were attracted to the area by its more peaceful and less polluted ambience and the cheaper rates. Their prosperity is evident from the contents of such as residences as Magdala House in Strandtown which were offered for sale in April 1875 by Martin Jaffé. The villa boasted three reception rooms and eleven bedrooms plus related exterior buildings. The sale included twelve leather dining chairs, rocking chairs, a Friedrich Ehrbar piano, two large gilt chimney glasses (mirrors), a girandole with glasses, walnut cabinets and inlaid loo table, Bergere furniture, a tapestry, carpets from Brussels and Kidderminster, mahogany Persian bedsteads, marble-top washstands, a five-light bronze gasalier, a landau 'in good order' and a refrigerator manufactured by Higgins of Cincinnati.

The growth of the district was exemplified by the construction of the Knockdene estate at the heart of Knock. The site was sold by the Ward family of Bangor in 1841 and became a fruit and vegetable nursery until it was sold in 1870, witnessing soon afterwards the construction of many prestigious villas. One of these, Astolat, was the home of John Milliken (see separate entry), one of the most respected worshippers at St Columba's, who was the long-serving Secretary of the Belfast & County Down Railway which ran close to his home. In addition to representing the railways, Milliken became involved in the wrangling of one other encroachment upon open land consequential upon an expanding population – the need for cemeteries!

In July 1896 he was one of the prime instigators of a meeting on behalf of "the residents, house– and property-owners of Knock" who were fearful of Belfast City Council's intention to build a cemetery on their doorstep. Milliken was a member of the deputation to the Old Town Hall to plead that the district "is a prosperous and growing one, already largely covered with villa residences, mainly of high valuation, and many of them recently created, the depreciation in the value of which, were a public cemetery established in their midst, would be immense". They also presented another financial plea: that they had recently suffered increased taxes because some of them were inside the newly-created city boundary – and, almost as an afterthought, threw in the argument that a cemetery at Knock was not a safe prospect on sanitary grounds.

Ultimately a compromise appears to have been reached, and a large cemetery opened in 1905 at Dundonald. Over the next few decades Dundonald was to play host to a very large number of local figures, including John Carey, the artist whose brother – J W Carey – had in sketched 1895 the fading relics of Conn O'Neill's castle, and local grocery entrepreneur Joseph Lowry Stewart (see separate entry). In common with Knock and Knockbreda cemeteries, Dundonald became the final resting place of victims of the First and Second World Wars. Knock graveyard features only one such distinctive headstone – that of Private John Corbett of Cuba Street, Ballymacarrett, who died on 9 March 1919 from the after-effects of war. Knockbreda cemetery and graveyard harbour 29 wartime victims, whilst Dundonald offers sanctuary to 76 soldiers of the First World War and 88 men and women from the second global conflict.

The latter list includes Pilot Officer Brian Stanley Bannister who was awarded a DFC in May 1941 "earned by conspicuous gallantry". The latter differed from the irascible Columba in that "one seldom saw [Bannister] in anything but a good temper". Nevertheless, all these men, and a multitude of others from the Knock district, echoed the restless, itinerant, courageous and adventurous character of the Irish saint. In the first half of the 9th century the German monk, Walafrid Strabo, had observed that, to the Irish people, "the custom of travelling to foreign lands has become almost second nature". Modern commentators have also identified this peripatetic trait:

> *... the idea of wandering became a part of the Celtic worldview. It was seen not only as a practical answer to troublesome conditions but also as a challenge and adventure, testing the character and the ingenuity of an individual. The idea of wandering took a central place in the lore of the Celts.*

In 1944 the retiring President of Wheaton College in Massachusetts advocated this wanderlust. John Edgar Park, the son of a prominent Presbyterian cleric, was raised and educated in the Knock locality at the close of the 19th century, but became an acknowledged educationalist in North America. He advocated to his audience that "You must have a touch of the Pilgrim Father in you. You must be going places".

One Belmont figure, a contemporary and obverse of Park, whose career – apart from brief service in the Boer War – was rooted firmly in the locality was that of Sir James Craig (later Lord Craigavon). With the establishment of the Cabinet Office briefly at Cabin Hill in 1921 and the opening of Stormont in 1932, Knock once again became the centre of the local political scene as it had been in the days of Conn O'Neill. The presiding hand was that of Craig and, although he may not have appreciated the analogy, one assessment of Columba could have applied equally to him: "He has come down the centuries as a cold hard man with his eye ever on the job".

Eccentrics

As host to an extensive base of professional and middle-class residences and, from 1932, to Stormont itself, the Knock district has, in recent times, exuded an air of solidity and self-assurance; yet over the centuries it has also experienced a turbulent and unsettled history and an enduring, if sporadic, historical tradition of characters who have proved non-conformist, idiosyncratic and eccentric.

Half a century after growing up in the area, Honor Atkinson (later Rudnitzky) formed the judgement that Knock "was not a very remarkable place. It was a quiet, respectable, middle-class neighbourhood … Yet, for all its sleepy tranquillity, I think Knock must have produced more oddities to the square acre than any other place on earth".

This assessment was inspired primarily by her memories of the family of the noted artist, J W Carey, on the Knockdene estate. For all his artistic talent and mental acuity – in 1922 he beat José Raúl Capablanca, world chess champion 1921-1927, at his own game – he was remarkably absent-minded and eccentric: during the high-security alerts of 1922 he was arrested trying to enter the grounds of neighbouring Cabin Hill – then the Cabinet Office – to remove dandelions from the lawns.

Some of their neighbours were equally unpredictable. 37 Cabin Hill Park was home to the five Mawhinney sisters who, according to one recollection, "specialised in running street battles in their nighties with china". In the 1920s a German named Frederick von Sparke, a naturalised citizen, lived at Lythe Bank (65 King's Road). He was married to an actress who allegedly glued her hair to her cheeks to keep it in place, and required painful surgery to repair the error of judgement. Next door, at no.67, lived the two Boyd sisters, daughters of St Clair Boyd of Ravenscroft House on North Road. Exceptionally wealthy, they lived a Spartan life-style, collecting silver paper, scavenging for firewood and cutting the grass with an ancient lawnmower whilst in their bare feet – explaining that this helped to preserve the pile of the lawn. They existed on damaged fruit, chipped eggs, fish and meat scraps, and hot water at bedtime – although their eccentricity did not adversely affect their health, as they died in the 1960s aged 89 and 91.

Some local clergymen exhibited tolerable foibles, such as the practice of James Hunter at Knock Presbyterian Church who endeavoured to delay the onset of puberty by placing benches between boys and girls at the Sunday School Christmas parties, whilst others possessed the less endearing qualities of Columba, being peevish and irascible and "always exploding about something". Rev Charles Inwood passed briefly through the district as minister at Knock Methodist Church (1894-1895), but still managed to alienate his congregation by accusing them of lacking "much out-and-out religion" and failing to understand the meaning of "holiness".

Some locals failed signally to control their tempers. On 26 March 1902 David Duncan of Knock, who was employed in the shipyards, hid his hatchet in a hedge on Barnett's Road after using it to attack his wife, Martha, with fatal results. In court he pleaded that "I didn't intend to kill her; it was done in a passion", but he did admit that he had taken drink to "embolden himself" after reflecting upon it for four years. Other women, however, were less inclined to accept a hierarchy within marriage: Alfred Baker, who lived at Trevena on Kensington Road at Knock, had painted the portraits of C S Lewis's father and of both his grandfathers and was regarded as "a local artist of some repute", but his wife was "a violent Suffragette".

Other wives were less fortunate in escaping tyranny. Joseph Greeves of Bernagh, one of the first villas built on Circular Road in Belmont, regularly reduced his wife to tears. He was an oppressive member of the Plymouth Brethren, "a harsh husband and a despotic father" (to four sons). C S Lewis, who maintained correspondence for a half-a-century with the youngest son, Arthur, revealed of the father that "In his declining years his habits became very gross, and I have heard that he commonly broke wind without restraint in the presence of his wife and children. My own father described his funeral as 'the most cheerful funeral he ever attended'". His third son, William Edward, took comfort in chocolate – on St Valentine's Day 1918 he married Marion Cadbury, heiress to the Bournville empire!

C S Lewis perhaps encapsulated the residents of the wider Knock area in the phrase – the only one which ever seems to have stumped his enduring editor, Walter Hooper – "These people are all so throughother"! It may not be, in Honor Rudnitzky's judgement, "a remarkable place", but Knock has certainly been home to some remarkable individuals.

L ALDEN
1869-1941

Although an Oxford man, Lewis Alden spent his entire school-teaching career in East Belfast. He was an inspirational and forward-thinking teacher to whom four eminent university professors were later to acknowledge their debt. He gave his name posthumously to a local restaurant.

Lewis Alden was born in Oxford on 11 June 1869, the fifth son of Isaac Alden, described as 'a gentleman'. The Aldens were a fertile clan, and Lewis himself had five brothers and at least one sister. The Alden family has long been established in the English university city, both as master butchers (whose trade still includes the stand of R R Alden in the famous covered market) and printers (in 1909 the Alden Group, established in 1832, published the first ever Oxford Guide). One of the family was Mayor of Oxford in 1936-1937.

Despite its comfortable prosperity, a vein of socialism and altruism ran through the family. One of Lewis's older brothers, Percy (born 1864), intended to become a Baptist minister, but his strong Christian commitment eventually encouraged him to adopt a political career. He was profoundly affected by social issues and reform, becoming a member of the Fabian Society. He was to influence Beveridge on the foundation of Labour Exchanges and to urge the provision of social housing, and wrote on such matters as unemployment. Supported by the philanthropist and reformer Seebohm Rowntree, Percy Alden became the Liberal MP for Tottenham between 1906 and 1918. His views on ethical socialism later encouraged him to convert to the Labour Party for whom he was briefly an MP between 1923 and 1924. His various charitable posts included that of Chairman of the Save the Children Fund. He was knighted in 1933 and died on 30 June 1944 on Tottenham Court Road in London as the result of a German bomb.

Lewis Alden typified the family's spirit of magnanimity. He was educated at Oxford High School before becoming an Exhibitioner at Wadham College, Oxford. There is no indication of his career prior to his arrival in 1898 at Campbell College, where he became Senior English Master.

One of the Best Schoolmasters

His character and contribution were encapsulated in a tribute composed shortly after his death:

> *He had a peculiar knack in drawing out the best that was in us. Very probably the chief claim to regard lay in the extraordinary kindness he always showed to the very small boys. To the problems of those of more mature generation he gave sympathetic and invariably wise advice. His ideals were the highest and nobody hated more than he any wilful departure from the pursuit of Honour ... Those who knew him at all intimately will bear witness to an extraordinary sense of humour which, itself an attribute of an inner calm and confidence, enabled him to bear without flinching a number of trials – especially in the last decade of his life – which would easily have daunted a less resolute though physically more robust man.*

One of his early pupils, J Ernest Davey, who became Professor of Church History at Presbyterian College in Belfast at the age of twenty-six, regarded Alden as "one of the best schoolmasters I have known" and recalled that "he was a man for whom literature lived and who was able to make it live for others. He made his subject interesting simply by being himself interested, by his own native love of great literature. His views were always his own, refreshing and honest, vivid, colourful and challenging".

Other pupils echoed this provocative style; one recalled that he would argue that, if thrown with sufficient force, a candle could pass through sheet steel. Some believed that he was easily distracted in class by 'red herrings', but the likelihood is that he actively elicited them. He ran a vigorous Debating Society, at which he encouraged pupils to adopt a dialectical stance. Two Campbell College pupils who became President of the Oxford Union in 1904 (Arthur Moore, later Editor of *The Statesman* in Calcutta) and 1907 (William Armour, later Editor of *The Northern Whig*) owed some of their debating skills to the practice they had enjoyed at the school. E R Dodds, later Regius Professor of Greek in Alden's home town, also acknowledged his personal debt to Lewis Alden:

> *"He was a man of real cultivation and widely-ranging interests. He taught me how to use words with discrimination, how to arrange a paragraph, how to argue in public without losing my head of my temper".*

Alden was well-versed in the more traditional and classical authors who have tended to dominate the curriculum. One memory placed him at his desk on a stormy October day: "When a gust of wind blew clouds of leaves past his window, he stood as though spellbound and recited [from Book I of Milton's *Paradise Lost*]: 'Thick as autumnal leaves that strow the banks in Vallombrosa'". His range of literary interest, however, was eclectic and bordered on the encyclopaedic. Harry Cronne, later a distinguished Professor Medieval History at Birmingham University, conceded that:

> *Alden was not a scholar ... but his love of English literature, especially poetry, was profound and he communicated it with gusto to his pupils. He delighted in reading to them at all ages, as they loved him to do. Even sophisticates of the Sixth [Form] enjoyed his organ recitals, as one might call them, of Milton and Matthew Arnold ... It was from Octie [Alden's nickname] that I first heard of A E Housman and listened to the sad, repetitive flute music of A Shropshire Lad. Alden made us aware of contemporary poetry, although he was very critical of a good deal of it, drumming impatiently upon his bald spot with spatulate fingers, as he tasted and rejected lines that fell short of his standards of prosody and intelligibility. He was very kind to little boys, encouraging them at first to read adventure stories, then enticing them on to classical examples and leading them, like the Pied Piper, to richer fields ... He early introduced me to the great Russian writers ... leavening the lump with the American humorists in whom he delighted.*

One other pupil – although only present at the school for ten weeks in late 1910 – who recalled the interpretation and magic of Matthew Arnold under Alden's tutelage was an 11-year-old C S Lewis: "Much the most important thing that happened to me at Campbell was that I there read *Sohrab and Rustum* in form under an excellent master whom we called Octie. I loved the poem at first sight and have loved it ever since". At QUB in 1915, Robert Wallace McConnell – who, within a year, lay dead on the battlefields of distant Mesopotamia – earned, in the words of his family, "a rare honour for a first-year man" by being awarded the Dufferin Medal for oratory. His knowledge of English literature was also viewed as unusually extensive, and this, his family added, was due primarily to Lewis Alden.

Alden also taught History and Religious Instruction – both of them viewed very much as subsidiary subjects. Alden sought to resolve the obligation and tedium of the latter by treating the Bible as literature. Cronne – who hailed from the manse at Katesbridge and then Portaferry – praised Alden's endeavours:

> *Most of the masters were probably unqualified for the chore of Scriptural teaching ... I do not recall that anyone other than 'Octie' Alden strove to make us appreciate the splendour of the Authorised Version as English prose, or made any real attempt to expound the historical, anthropological, sociological, military or other aspects of the Scriptures that might have been made interesting.*

The teaching of History was usually done by rote in the early twentieth century, and Alden's teaching of this subject lacked inspiration, but he recommended the reading of passages, character sketches and famous passages from Gibbon and Macaulay, which he regarded as good literature. Another pupil, sixty years later, recalled that the Senior English Master was accustomed to employ the volume Deeds that Won the Empire (probably in the 1909 version, adapted for use in schools).

Octie

When, occasionally, he was roused to anger, Lewis Alden harboured a legendary temper, described variously as 'choleric' and 'volcanic'. It was this that prompted the sobriquet 'Octie', as Harry Cronne explained,""because his eyes swelled like those of an octopus when he was angry" – although he did add the caveat: "if this is indeed zoological fact".

The prevailing mould in which he was cast, however, was – as Ernest Davey categorised it – "warm-hearted, understanding, sensitive, affectionate and wise ... he was at once honest, humble, lovable and spontaneous ... indeed, to know him was in itself a liberal education". Harry Cronne perhaps couched it in more romantic terms: "Normally he looked, and was, a benevolent old gentleman, with his white hair and kindly smile beneath downward sweeping moustaches ... to the boys he appeared a venerable personage –

Father Christmas without the beard". Even beyond the classroom the Oxford man impressed. Clarke MacDermott, later Lord Chief Justice of Northern Ireland, was a pupil at Campbell College between 1907 and 1914; he recalled that: "Skating [on Netherleigh lake] revealed him to many small boys like myself as an even more accomplished person than we had thought him to be. He skated with speed and confidence, with body erect and a great cigar in his mouth".

The Senior English Master demonstrated his generosity in many ways. Both Ernest Davey and Eric Dodds recorded their gratitude at the privilege he accorded them – and others – of the unlimited use of his extensive personal library. As one might expect in an institution that marketed itself on its hygiene and sanitation, there was plenty of water available to the boys for purposes of washing. Unfortunately much of it was cold, so illicit access to the hot water available to the resident Staff was pursued. One bathroom in the boarding area belonged jointly to two masters – John William Yates (a Birmingham man) and Robert Knox McElderry (an Ulsterman). One morning Yates found himself locked out of his own bathroom and, hearing splashing, he asked who was in the bath. A reluctant voice, featuring the pronounced southern accent of the occupant, eventually answered: "Me, sur". Yates asked who "Me" was and, after a further delay, the reluctant voice responded: "Mr McElderry, sir"! Harry Cronne recalled that he and a friend also regularly acquired hot water from Alden's bathroom, and marvelled: "I cannot imagine why neither of us was ever caught as we passed to and fro with a steaming bedroom jug in each hand, for concealment was quite impossible". One suspects that the schoolmaster simply turned a blind eye.

This was not entirely inapposite for, despite the voluminous amount of reading which Alden consumed, he had to wear thick pince-nez to compensate for extreme myopia. He admitted that this had once caused him serious difficulty when, being a strong swimmer, he had once "swum far out to sea, when a wave removed his pince-nez and left him quite unable to tell where the land lay".

Award-winning

The respect in which he was held at Campbell was demonstrated by his being appointed one of the original eponymous Housemasters in 1908. He was also asked to deputise as Acting Headmaster during the inter-regnum following the death of the incumbent Headmaster in April 1922, and was to be praised publicly during Speech Day three months later "for all he had done in taking up the reins and carrying on the work of the school". He would have been expected, in accordance with the regulations of the Board of Governors, to retire at the age of sixty in the summer of 1929, but was given an extension of a year. Upon his retirement in 1930, after 32 years at Campbell College, he was provided by the Board with a supplementary annual pension of £38.

At the start of the 1941-1942 academic year (when the school was in residence at Portrush) Alden had written to say that "but for twinges of neuritis caused by a fall down the steps of his front door, he was in the best of health". He passed away suddenly, however, on 22 October 1941. No less an author than C S Lewis wrote, fourteen years later, "on Octie be peace". It is likely that, as former pupils reminisced when, in the 1920s and 1930s, they met by chance in distant places such as the hill stations of Gulmarg in the Kashmir, or at St Patrick's Day gatherings in Mumbai, Lewis Alden's name featured prominently.

In 1998 Lewis Alden's name became immortalised in East Belfast. Erstwhile Campbell College pupil, Jonathan Davis, a member of Alden's House, went into business at Ballyhackamore, and opened what rapidly became an award-winning restaurant – which he named 'Alden's'. It has since been renamed the 'Neill's Hill' bistro.

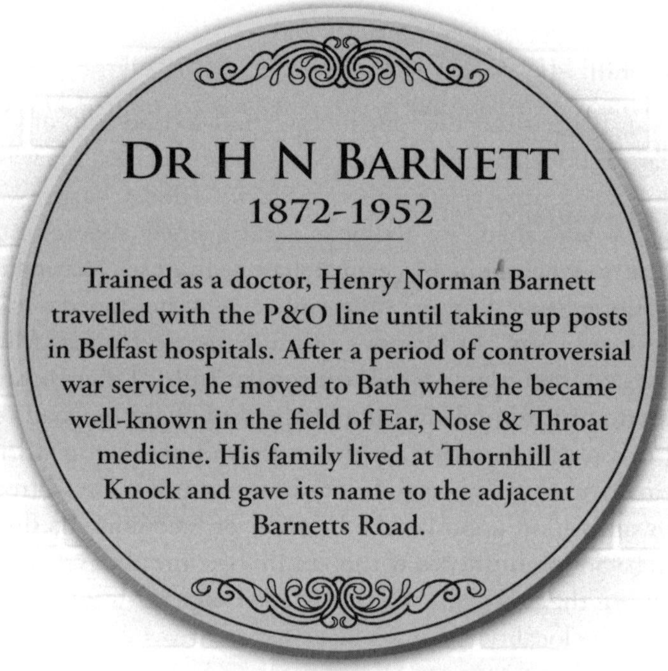

Norman Barnett and his family could boast a number of notable ancestors and relations. The Barnetts arrived in Ireland from Warwickshire in the final years of the 17th century, settling in the townland of Ballyagherty in the parish of Saintfield. Richard Barnett – Norman's great-grandfather, buried in the graveyard of Saintfield Parish Church – was an apothecary in the town and set the precedent for the medical profession in which a number of them were to practise. They appear to have remained a close-knit clan, and when spinster Mary Barnett (of 151 Botanic Road, off Great Victoria Street) died on 18 March 1867, the administration of her estate was given to her nephew and "one of the next of kin", Charles William Barnett, who was described as a merchant of Belfast.

Thornhill

Norman Barnett was the fourth child, and second son, of Charles William and Helen Limmie (née Mackenzie) Barnett. He was born in Holywood on 16 September 1872. By 1880 Charles William Barnett – who made his living as a yarn, linen and commission agent at 8 Wellington Place in Belfast – lived at Nottinghill on the Malone Road, but on 5 September 1884 he signed a lease for 9900 years, at £82 6s 9d per annum, with Sir Thomas McClure for the six acres on the Upper Newtownards Road that constituted the estate of Thornhill in the townland of Ballycloughan – with the proviso that he maintain the roads and paths in good repair. Originally named Thornyhill, the Georgian house dated from the 1780s and stood opposite the location of Stormont Presbyterian Church. So established did the family become there that, before the end of the century, it had christened such by-ways as Barnetts Road in the locality.

Charles William Barnett, who died on 11 September 1887, had four children – two daughters and two sons (Charles Mackenzie and Henry Norman). By the time that his mother died on 12 May 1912, Norman was the only surviving offspring. His brother was an electrical engineer who had been living in London at the turn of the century, and who had died (aged about 35) following a brief illness on 20 March 1904 at the rectory in Granard, Co Longford; his body was returned to Belfast by train from Cavan. Norman's affection for his mother – who attended St Columba's Church after it opened on 13 June 1896 – is manifested in the dedication to her of his *Student's Textbook of Surgery* of 1916.

Medicine

Norman Barnett was educated at Belfast Royal Academy and in Brighton, before studying medicine at Queen's College in Belfast and subsequently in Edinburgh, where he qualified in 1898. His choice of career may well have been influenced by the presence of close relations in the medical profession (John Milford Barnett and Richard Barnett) who lived in Holywood.

Norman Barnett was elected a member of the North of Ireland branch of the British Medical Association on 26 January 1899, when he was listed as being resident at Thornhill. Before he settled to a more traditional medical career, he appears to have travelled extensively. One source states that he had visited India, China, Japan, the Straits Settlement, Australia, South Africa and the United States, but some – or all – of this was probably a consequence of his appointment to the P&O shipping line.

His personal experience at sea was the inspiration for a couple of his early books: *Guide to an Eastern ocean voyage* and *Sea Sickness: its true cause and cure*. He recorded his presence on board a ship as it left Bombay, only to encounter very quickly the South West Monsoon. He recalled that the seas were mountainous:

> *Add to this heavy rain; a moist, hot atmosphere, almost unbearable in the cabins; the moral effect of the tremendous noise of the elements, alternating with the crash of china or woodwork as delf or fixtures are broken; the rattle of chains; the distant thunder of the engines; now and again the thud of running feet overhead ... nothing to be seen but green water surging against the porthole.*

He believed of sea-sickness that "There is no minor ailment ... which causes so much discomfort, none which gains so little sympathy from those unaffected by it, and has had such divergent prescribing with so little good result". He combined direct observation, such as the fact that many retired to lower-deck cabins where "the atmosphere of such a cabin teems with tubercle bacilli and other forms of germ life inimical to health", with a plea for more rational remedies, as most are prescribed "by men who have had no practical experience of what real sea-sickness is, nor of the varying complications likely to arise".

At Queen's College, Belfast (as it was then called) he came under the supervision and influence of the noted lecturer in ophthalmology, Cecil Edward Shaw, who also specialised in diseases of the ear and throat. During the first decade of the 20th century Barnett published several medical works, the first of which, *Accidental Injuries to Workmen*, prepared on the heels of the Workmen's Compensation Act of 1906, included a section written by Shaw relating to "the organs of special sense". The publication highlighted the nascent official concern with national welfare and well-being: "As time goes on there is an ever-increasing desire on the part of the Home Office to increase the number of diseases in respect of which compensation is payable", and the physician observed that accidental injury to workers required better consideration and "when fully appreciated will lead employers to be more particular as to the physical fitness of those whom they engage".

Barnett himself eventually also specialised in otorhinolarynology, reflected in further publications such as *Deafness: its Cause and Treatment* and *Mastoiditis: its Diagnosis and Treatment*. Whilst working in Belfast up to the outbreak of the First World War – with a residence (and possibly a surgery) at 1 College Square East – he held the posts of Surgical Assistant at the Belfast Hospital for Sick Children and at the Ulster Hospital for Diseases of the Eye, Ear, Nose & Throat, and he was also a surgeon at the Cripples Institute for Ireland. Additionally, he acted as Surgeon, Registrar and Tutor, Anaesthetist and Resident Clinical Assistant at the Royal Victoria Hospital.

The Problems of Alcohol

The Introduction to his *Student's Textbook of Surgery* hints at Barnett's attachment to the antique medical principles of Hippocrates and Galen. He advises his readers that, although there have been many contemporary developments in such as pathology, bacteriology and antisepsis, nothing can properly replace direct clinical observation of the patient and his/her illness and he adds: "the modern surgeon ... must, to be truly successful, be a man of wide culture, a highly-developed brain and a sympathetic nature".

Nevertheless, in spite of this traditionalist vein, Norman Barnett exhibited a modern approach to medical issues and problems. One topic in which he showed an early interest was that of drunkenness. Intoxication was an endemic social problem at all levels of society, with often severe economic consequences. A survey in 1836 indicated that throughout Belfast, including Ballymacarrett, there were at least 750 outlets selling alcohol. Even after Barnett's departure to England there were those in East Belfast attempting to deal with the problem. Rev John Redmond, the rector of St Patrick's (1920-1929) in Ballymacarrett – a church which the doctor will have travelled past on many occasions – was vainly to hope that the new Northern Ireland Government would successfully tackle the problem. He recorded that in the early 1920s there were over 125 outlets serving alcohol in the Mountpottinger locality alone.

Barnett adopted a more sympathetic and practical approach towards dealing with the problem, as outlined in his two booklets: *Drunkenness: Sin or Disease?* (1907) and *Legal Responsibility of the Drunkard* (1908). The doctor argued that there were a variety of social and environmental, in addition to personal, causes of drunkenness, and that in its advanced stages it was necessary to treat it as a disease, as "we have in the drunkard one whom we know by observation, by experiment and by the pathology of the nervous system, to be suffering from a definite nerve-lesion, one whose responsibility for crime may well be doubted".

He believed that magistrates were unable to deal effectively with the problem. He was contemptuous of the fact that publicans, who would lose the custom of a gaoled inebriate – "much too good a one to lose by his going to prison even for a short period" – were allowed to pay the fines of customers charged with drunkenness on their premises. If an habitual drunk were imprisoned, Barnett argued, his wife and children would starve, and may then be added to the burden of the public purse by being placed in the workhouse. When the drunkard was released, his craving for alcohol would be such that he was likely to re-offend immediately – thus creating a vicious circle. Norman Barnett argued that remedial treatment should be legally obligatory. He propounded a totally new approach, as "Our present system of dealing with the drunkard has failed lamentably, for it is based on the wrong assumption ... Is it not time that such a system be abolished and one founded on a scientific and moral basis put in its place?"

Bath

Sometime between April and June 1910 Barnett married (in Kensington, London) Jane Eleanor Shaw, daughter of Thomas Shaw of Lancashire. Barnett remained responsive to the politics of his native province; on 28 September 1912 he showed himself willing to queue at Belfast City Hall to sign the Solemn League & Covenant against Home Rule. Whilst resident at Thornhill, as did his mother, Norman Barnett probably worshipped at St Columba's Church, and he was a lay member of the Synod of the Church of Ireland. The death of his mother, however, in May 1912 effectively ended his last close family tie to the Knock district, and on 10 April 1913 Cecil Edward Shaw passed away before his fiftieth birthday. It may have been these shocks which persuaded Norman Barnett to pursue another post. In 1915 Thornhill was listed as vacant.

By 1916 he lived at 27 The Circus in Bath, an address he still owned at the time of his death. He became Surgeon at the Bath Ear, Nose & Throat Hospital, and at the Ear, Nose & Throat War Hospital – an institution which he effectively established – and also held the related post of Consulting Surgeon for Diseases of the

Ear, Nose & Throat at the Bath Officers' Convalescent Home. This work, however, was to be disrupted by his wartime service.

For a year prior to the outbreak of the Boer War (1898-1899) he had served in the Regular RAMC, and during the conflict (1899-1900) he had undertaken some transport and trooping duties. Subsequently he was placed on the Reserve List. On 2 March 1914 he joined – with the rank of Captain – 2 South-Western Mounted Brigade Field Ambulance (SWMBFA), and was serving with this unit on Salisbury Plain when war was declared on 4 August 1914. He attained temporary promotion to the rank of Major on 5 January 1915, and three months later was instructed to raise, train and command 3/2 SWMBFA until its personnel were posted to the regular RAMC. A year later he was in command of units 3/1 and 3/2 SWMBFA.

In November 1916 he was appointed Assistant Commandant of the RAMC Training Centre at Codford in Wiltshire. It was a posting which he was reluctant to take but, before he had time to argue his case, he was suddenly posted on 3 January 1917 to 2/3 West Riding Field Ambulance in 62 Division – which he claimed must have been a mistake! On 21 January his commanding officer asked for Barnett's rank of Major to be re-confirmed as "he is a very valuable asset to this unit, especially as all the other officers are of comparatively junior service". From January to early June 1917 he served with this unit in France but, although he was placed temporarily in command when his commanding officer was evacuated when sick, he never rose officially above the rank of Captain.

Barnett believed this was an injustice and it clearly rankled for a long time. In June he returned to England suffering from Trench Fever and from his home in Bath on 4 July – explaining that "I am now at home convalescing ... [and] have been in bed for a month and am awfully weak" – he summoned the strength to urge a friend's intervention. He evidently believed that his professional and specialist surgical experience on the staff of a teaching hospital, combined with the publication of his *Textbook* in 1916, merited a more responsible position. Having been placed in temporary command of his unit in France and "being told to get a bad Unit efficient in the shortest possible time", someone else with less experience had been appointed over his head. Consequently, from his sick-bed, he complained that "I have grievance and ask for its redress". The disappointing explanation was that he could only be promoted to Major within the same unit in which he had originally served – and that that was now defunct! He did eventually receive some satisfaction on 25 March 1918 when it was conceded that from 24 February to 30 March 1917 he was entitled to "the acting rank of Lieut-Colonel". He continued to quibble, however, and one official internal memorandum of 28 June 1918 – with some irritation evident in the split infinitive! – pleaded: "Can any action be taken to definitely terminate this correspondence, please?"!

The rest of his wartime career consisted of a series of short-term appointments. Captain Barnett was sent back to France in September 1917, but soon after was given command of the Chiseldon Venereal Disease Hospital near Swindon. He was ordered overseas again on 11 February 1918 when he was appointed Officer Commanding No.2 General Hospital of the BEF in France, only to return to London on 26 April. Seven weeks later Captain Barnett RAMC assumed command of the 750-bed Warlingham Military Hospital in south London – although on this occasion he was given from the outset the acting rank of Lieut-Colonel, which he was eventually relinquish on 10 November 1919, six days before his demobilisation. It is unclear whether Barnett was held responsible, or whether it was a condition which he inherited, but in July 1919 the Secretary of State for War (Winston Churchill) was asked in the House of Commons if he were aware "that a very serious state of affairs exists at the military hospital for venereal diseases at Warlingham; that the hospital is understaffed and the supervision of the men inadequate; ... that thefts are frequent, and that, owing to insufficient guard, patients break bounds whenever they wish, cutting the barbed wire and violently assaulting those who try to restrain them ... [and that] the discipline of soldiers on guard is much impaired".

Norman Barnett thereafter lived and worked in Bath, maintaining his specialism in otorhinolarynology, encapsulated by his volume entitled *The Approach of the General Practitioner to Diseases of the Ear, Nose & Throat*. He was in later years appointed Consulting Specialist to the Ministries of Pensions and of National Insurance, and in this capacity, writing in the December 1950 issue of *Medical World*, he was critical of the indiscriminate prescription of deaf aids (under the recently introduced National Health Service) by "persons with little qualification to judge their need and without ascertaining whether the patient would derive any benefit". He defined the practice as altruistic but ill-advised, and challenged Aneurin Bevan (the first Minister of Health) as "merely a political propagandist who sees in it a piece of vote-catching machinery".

Dr Norman Barnett died on 24 April 1952 at South Lynn, Weston Road, Bath, a few months short of his eightieth birthday. His links with his native province had apparently not been totally severed for his effects in Northern Ireland were listed as totalling £3769 18s 3d. He had one son and two daughters.

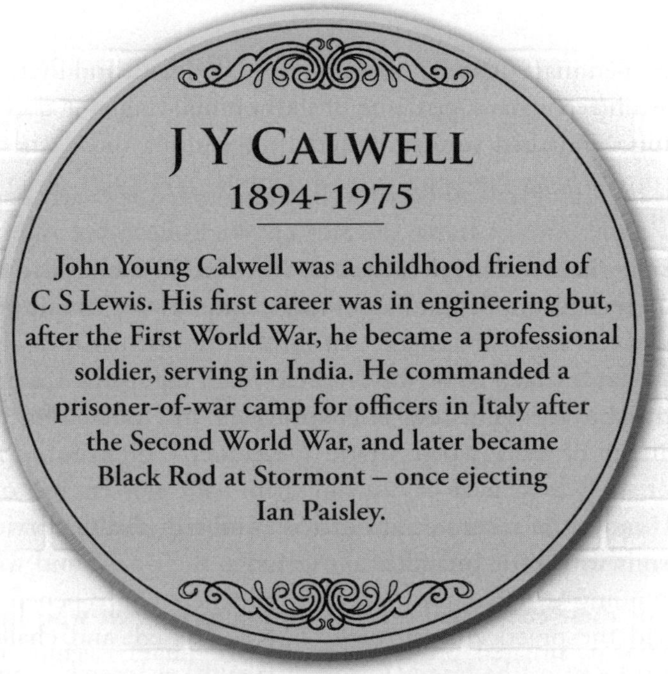

Jack Calwell was one of a considerable number of individuals from East Belfast who were to take advantage of the opportunities offered by the British Empire. Although his education inculcated the military and imperial traditions which encouraged such aspirations, the lure of the Orient was already entrenched amongst the Belfast mercantile community.

One future Professor of Medieval History, also educated in East Belfast, later asserted that "The City Fathers in the early years of the twentieth century, already installed in the present Mughal Palace [i.e. City Hall], from which the gorgeous East might have been held in fee, were presiding over a booming metropolis of linen, shipbuilding and engineering". The representation of Belfast City Hall as a Mughal palace was not an affectation. It was appropriate that the Victoria Memorial in Calcutta – for which the foundation stone was laid in the same year as the completion of

Donegall Square (1906) – should reflect, at least partially, Mughal architecture, but a comparison of the two buildings will also reveal a distinct similarity in their design.

Ships built by Harland & Wolff had long sailed regularly between Belfast and ports in India; the Sirocco Works designed and manufactured virtually all the industrial machinery used in the Indian tea trade; and the Belfast Ropework Company and the Robinson & Cleaver store had many customers in the East, including Maharajahs. Much of the trade of the latter company was centred upon linen products, and linen provided the foundation of the prosperity of a large percentage of families – often inter-related – in East Belfast, even if most of them were not on the scale of the Ewart (as at Glenmachan and Schomberg) and Greeves (as at Bernagh, Tweskard and Altona) dynasties.

One of these individuals was John Young Calwell who lived at Woodlawn, situated on the bend of Sydenham Avenue, opposite Strathearn. He had married Fanny, the daughter of William Roberston, who lived a mile distant in the grandeur of Netherleigh. His two sons were educated in the locality; the elder, William, died in 1910 at the age of 21, but the younger son – born on 24 March 1894 (accompanied by his twin sister, Jane) and who assumed his father's full name – survived to be an octogenarian. John Young Calwell junior served in India (and elsewhere), but died in 1975 whilst living barely a third of a mile from the home where he had been born and raised – which was still in family hands, occupied by his sister (who died in 1976) and a niece.

Entertainment

About the age of eleven he became friendly with C S Lewis and his brother, who moved in 1905 to Circular Road, a very short distance from his home. The social cohesion of the Belmont and Knock district appears to have remained quite strong; at the end of

1922 the younger Lewis felt it worth recording in his diary that, on his way back home from lunch at the McNeills on Belmont Road, he had encountered Mrs Calwell in the street. The voluminous correspondence of the creator of Narnia provides some insight into the pastimes and playtime of the Belmont middle-classes, and towards the end of 1905 Lewis – then approaching seven years of age – observed to his brother that "Diabolos are all the go here, everybody has one except us. I don't think the Lewis temper would hold out, do you? Jackie Calwell has one and can do it beautifully (wish I could)".

Amongst the older generations Bridge was commonly played, but relief from cards was found in a form of literary charades, as played just before Christmas 1914 at Glenmachan, when the participants performed titles of books to be guessed. The latter occasion was organised by Kelso, the daughter of Sir William Ewart, who clearly used such occasions to nurture her inveterate penchant for gossiping, an essential art of the idle rich. Seven years later, Lewis (whose nickname for her was 'the Valkyrie') met her for dinner in Oxford and reported that "On this occasion, honestly it was so boring that there was an air of insanity about it all ... She never paused. Stories that I heard from those same lips so often before followed one another". Nevertheless, such irritation did not obliterate the enchantment in the future Oxford don's memories; he recalled: "I think we Strandtown and Belmont people had among us as much kindness, wit, beauty and taste as any circle of the same size that I have ever known".

Musical evenings were also popular, either communally in church halls or more intimately in private homes. Some years later (after he had sold the family home) Lewis was to express nostalgia for such occasions. One of the most popular hosts was James Armstrong Thompson who lived across the road from the Calwells at Penrhyn (which is now the junior department of Strathearn School) and in

1931 Lewis reminisced: "Once more to spend one of our delightful banjo evenings with Jimmy Thompson".

A Military Man

When war erupted in 1914, it was service at the Front which seems to have persuaded Jack Calwell about his choice of career. Upon leaving school in July 1911 he worked briefly for the engineering company, W R MacColl & Co, based near Queen's Quay in the heartland of industrial Ballymacarrett. His family was committed to the Unionist resistance to Home Rule – the management of which was conducted only a half-a-mile from his home at Craigavon House – in the years before the First World War. His father had queued along with his neighbour, Jimmy Thompson, to sign the Solemn League & Covenant in 1912 at their place of worship, St Mark's Church on the Holywood Road, and young Jack enlisted in the UVF.

As with so many of his contemporaries, it was a natural progression to the ranks of 36 (Ulster) Division. He was commissioned as a 2nd Lieut on 23 June 1915, probably in 8 Battalion (East Belfast Volunteers) of the Royal Irish Rifles. He was promoted to Lieut on 1 January 1917, becoming a Temporary Captain only six days later, and in October of that year suffered both wounds and gas poisoning. He relinquished the rank in July 1918 when he left his battalion, but it would appear that he had then determined on a permanent military career. In 1919 he was serving with the Army of Occupation in Europe, but by 1922 he was a Captain in the newly-formed Royal Ulster Rifles (RUR). Subsequently he was based at Poona (now Pune) and the North-West Frontier in India and on 13 July 1935 was appointed a Member of the Royal Victorian Order (MVO), probably for services in India.

In 1933 he was Assistant Provost Marshal, in charge of the Royal Military Police, at Aldershot and, upon being appointed a Major in the RUR in late 1935, was transferred to the same role in Palestine & Transjordan. By 1940 he was serving with 50 Division in the Western and was appointed a Lieut-Colonel on 24 May 1941. He became a Brigadier in 1943 during his campaigns in Sicily and Italy, and subsequently on 19 April 1945 he was awarded the CBE "in recognition of gallant and distinguished services in Italy". He was mentioned in despatches on four occasions.

In 1947 Calwell was placed in command of the Riccione-Rimini camp in north-eastern Italy which housed some prominent Axis prisoners after the Second World War. From mid-January 1947 Feldmarschall Albert Kesselring was held there in preparation for his trial at a British military court in Venice, which lasted from February until May 1947, and he was accompanied each day by Calwell. Many of those held at the camp much longer than Kesselring wrote to the East Belfast man to express their gratitude for his considerate and courteous treatment of them. Kesselring was equally generous in his appreciation of Calwell's disposition and, in an oblique nod to the latter – which had a direct bearing upon his conduct in his role at Stormont – wrote in his autobiography (Soldat bis zum letzten Tag): "It did me good in such short moments to see that camaraderie did not stop at borders or before the conquered. I am repeatedly glad to see those soldiers are often better, more emphatic politicians than those who feel themselves called to politics".

He retired from the RUR as an Honorary Brigadier in February 1948, but was their Chief Recruiting Officer until he was appointed Black Rod and Deputy Serjeant-at-Arms in the Northern Ireland Parliament at Stormont in 1954. The military expertise and experience appears almost to have been a prerequisite for the posts: his predecessor since 1921 had been Brigadier Thomas Hackett, and in 1968 he succeeded Brigadier Nelson Russell as Serjeant-at-Arms. (By a strange coincidence, both Hackett and Russell had been fellow pupils at Campbell College). One obituary claimed that "He was a mine of information about many of the great names in the Army and had many amusing stories to tell about some of his experiences in Stormont", but unfortunately these were not recorded – except for the fact that he had to eject a truculent Rev Ian Paisley from the chamber on the 280th anniversary of the Battle of the Boyne (1 July 1970)!

His charitable services were honoured in June 1956 when he was appointed as a Commander of the Most Venerable Order of the Hospital of St John of Jerusalem; his fellow appointees on that date included Viscount Curzon, J Arthur Rank and another former fellow pupil, Surgeon Rear-Admiral Richard Proctor. In the early 1950s he had resided at Helen's Bay but, at the time of his death in the Ulster Hospital on 11 October 1975, he had lived for some time at 62 Circular Road very close to his childhood home. He appears to have been a frugal man, leaving the considerable sum of £75,000 which, apart from a gift of £500 to his sister, he divided between the latter's three children.

C D CHASE
1878-1965

Always known as 'Chevy', Chase spent 60 years at Campbell College, inevitably becoming a 'Mr Chips' figure – which was itself a strange coincidence, as the man he replaced at his first teaching post was the very model for the original 'Mr Chips'. Chase became a noted naturalist and botanist and President of the Belfast Naturalists' Field Club.

The longest-serving member of the staff at Campbell College was Albert Maxwell, who retired as Head Porter in 1993 after 64 years of unbroken full-time service. Amongst the academic staff, however, Corrie Denew Chase – universally known at Belmont as 'Chevy' – was the schoolmaster whose name was associated most enduringly (60 years) with the institution.

He was born on 12 August 1878 at Weston-super-Mare, where his father (Rev Charles Henry Chase) was curate to his own father (Rev Henry John Neale Chase). One of Corrie Chase's great-grandfathers, Samuel Chase, had been Mayor of Reading in 1842, but their genealogical inheritance primarily encompassed members of the professions: medical and legal, plus many ecclesiastical figures, boasting two Bishops of the Church of England (Frederic Henry Chase, Bishop of Ely 1905-1924, and his son, George Armitage Chase, Bishop of Ripon 1946-1959). Additionally, a nephew, Michael White, became a world expert in animal cytogenetics and a Fellow of the Australian Academy of Science. In 1882 Corrie Chase went to live in the Lake District when his father obtained the incumbency of Ambleside. A clerical neighbour was Rev Hardwicke Drummond Rawnsley, the founder of The National Trust, whose interests and writings in nature, botany and rambling ultimately may well have exercised some influence upon the young Chase.

In 1891 Corrie's father became Rector of St Minver (near Wadebridge) on the north Cornish coast and, after a very brief period at a prep school near Malvern, the fourteen-year-old was sent for his education to Blundell's School in Devon in 1892. Here he was raised in the prevailing philosophy of 'manliness' or 'muscular Christianity' – so avidly introduced at Campbell College by its second Headmaster, R A H MacFarland (1908-1922) – which sought to combine the ideals of a Christian ethos with athleticism. Corrie readily participated in the principal sports of rugby and cricket, and excelled at gymnastics, but was also sufficiently scholastic to earn a scholarship to Sidney Sussex College at Cambridge (1897-1900).

Campbell College

Upon graduation he started in September 1900 as a Classics master at Woodbridge School in Suffolk. At some stage he determined to pursue an interest in Modern Languages, and in 1903 resigned and spent the next two years studying German at Heidelberg University and French at the Sorbonne in Paris. Possibly as a result of his acquaintance with his Sidney Sussex contemporary, George Ritchie Thompson – one of the first pupils at Campbell College in 1894, who returned to become a member of staff in 1900 – Corrie Chase took up a post as a Modern Languages teacher at Belmont in 1905. He was appointed Senior Modern Languages Master in 1911, a post he held until his official retirement in 1938. In the years before the First World War, Chase encouraged familiarity with languages by taking small groups of pupils on visits to the continent during the summer vacation, and even translated nursery rhymes such as *Jack and Jill* and *Baa, baa, Black Sheep* into French.

Soldier

Chase was closely involved in the formation of the Campbell College OTC in late 1909 – the first school contingent in Ireland – and, as its Commanding Officer, organised regular Field Days, shooting practices and camps in England. Despite the fact that, as an Englishman, he may have felt that the struggles of Ulstermen against Home Rule were not his problem, he signed the Solemn League & Covenant (September 1912) at Campbell College, in company with a number of colleagues. When the European war erupted in August 1914 he enlisted in the Royal Irish Rifles, being appointed a Captain in no.3 Company of 16 (Pioneer) Battalion, alongside his Campbell colleague, William Henry Madden. He was presented by the Headmaster with an inscribed pair of binoculars, which are still in the family's possession. After being transported to France in October 1915, his unit was based near Raincheval, just behind the Somme front. Over the winter months, in appalling weather, Chase led his Company in constructing trenchworks and dugouts, often within 200 yards of the German lines.

During the first five months of 1916 Chase and no.3 Company were intensively engaged in the construction of a 20-mile, full-gauge railway from Candas to Acheux, close to the front lines. On 19 June he was temporarily appointed second-in-command of the Pioneer Battalion. Chase was actively involved when the Battle of the Somme erupted on 1 July, and the Battalion War Diary records that, at the end of the day: "Capt Chase showed great calmness and military skill in helping to make arrangements for holding our first line lest the enemy should attack. All Thiepval Wood was under heavy shell fire and the scene is beyond description". On 3 July his Company succeeded in cutting the only trench to be laid across no-man's-land. Later in the year Capt Madden recorded in a letter to Campbell College that his colleague had "had a lucky escape as he was returning from the line when the strafe started, and [Chase] is said to have beaten even time in the last hundred yards".

In May 1917 he was mentioned in the despatches of Field Marshal Haig, and two months later moved with his Company near Poperinghe to the west of Ypres. He became briefly involved in the early stages of the Third Battle of Ypres (or Passchendaele), before returning to the Somme sector in late August. Three months later he was assigned to the General Staff List, and was awarded the Military Cross on 1 January 1918 which *The Campbellian* magazine claimed was for "conspicuous gallantry in the field", although Chase always claimed it was a 'routine' award. He was eventually demobilised on 1 February 1919, when he returned to teaching duties at Campbell College.

Schoolmaster

During the 1920s he became one of the boarding Housemasters, and unsuccessfully applied for the Headmastership in 1922. As head of the languages department he was probably involved in the brief engagement of Samuel Beckett at Campbell during the first half of 1928. In many ways 'Chevy' Chase typified the traditional, conservative approach to schoolmastering. He adopted a very frugal life-style, although this was often typical of his profession. Teaching was very badly rewarded between the Wars, with pay cuts not unknown, and some of his colleagues suffered a precarious financial existence. He was known for his spartan wardrobe. When travelling abroad for several weeks during the summer vacation, apart from the clothes he travelled in, he regarded one additional shirt and one pair of socks as adequate luggage. Whatever the weather, until his later years, he never donned a raincoat and within the school buildings he almost invariably wore carpet slippers.

He never learned to drive, and could walk prodigious distances. When visiting the centre of Belfast, Chase would usually walk between the Belmont and the city, which took him through the economically depressed parts of East Belfast, the problems and realities of which seem to have eluded him. Committed to the academic life, much of his private time was spent in reading. At his funeral it was said: "His bookshelves were tightly packed. Here there was evidence of judicious selection and planned reading ... His tastes lay mainly among the well-tried classics, for he had no use for the ephemeral and catch-penny. He was a good scholar, sound in classical languages and widely read in several modern ones". As he wandered through Ballymacarrett, Chase could not comprehend why so many men gathered pointlessly on street corners or at the entrance to public houses: "How far better these men would be employed", he suggested in 1930, "had they some rational interest in life, some hobby, which would take them out into the open country to study the works of nature; or if they were to remain quietly at home reading some work of philosophy, Kant's *Critique of Pure Reason*, for example, or Dante's *Divine Comedy*, or even – shall we say – their Bibles?"

When, as a consequence of the school regulations, he was obliged to retire at the age of sixty in 1938, he asked to be allowed to stay on at Belmont "on the understanding that his services should not involve the Governors in any financial liability". This was accepted, and when seventeen members of the Campbell Staff enlisted on the outbreak of the Second World War and the College was evacuated to the Northern Counties Hotel in Portrush in late 1940, Chase's continued service proved invaluable. In August 1943, at the age of 65, he was legally obliged to retire, but he offered to teach without salary in return for board and lodging. He returned with the College upon its resettlement at Belmont in February 1946, and continued to teach part-time, offering tuition to those entering public examinations (particularly Oxbridge) and nature study classes in the school grounds to junior classes.

Botanist

The latter stemmed from his enduring interest in natural history. There is evidence that Chase began collecting botanical specimens before the First World War, when he was encouraged to assist his colleague, Stephen Bennett, in cataloguing the flora of the Belmont estate. In 1919 Chase joined the Belfast Naturalists' Field Club (BNFC), and rapidly became a highly respected and very active member. He botanised widely, taking the opportunity to gather plants at all locations – on the Campbell College estate, at rubbish tips, in gravel pits, by the side of railways lines, at Ballykinlar Camp, and particularly along the north Antrim coast during the school's sojourn in Portrush. After his lengthy summer holidays abroad he would present exhibitions at the annual BNFC *Conversazioni*, and gave numerous public lectures. In 1927, during his Presidential address, R S Lepper declared that Chase's "wide knowledge of the plants of Ulster, of Europe generally, and even of other continents, bade fair to become encyclopaedic".

The Englishman's botanical expertise was respected by all the other leading figures of the period, such as Robert Lloyd Praeger of Holywood who, in 1949, included Chase in his collection *Some Irish Naturalists: biographical note-book*, in which he conceded that: "[Chase] is an excellent field botanist, and has done useful work in the north-east. His holidays have been spent mostly on the continent and in North Africa, where he has carried out widespread herborisations". He was especially adept at discovering alien plant species in Ireland. Chase contributed a number of articles to the *Irish Naturalists' Journal*, and is listed amongst the Principal Collectors and Recorders in S A Stewart and T H Corry's essential volume: *Flora of the North East of Ireland*. His personal Herbarium of (it is claimed) approximately 4000 specimens is now held by the Ulster Museum.

In 1930 he was elected President of the BNFC, a post which had been held in 1922 by his colleague, Stephen Bennett. Following the initial impulse given by the latter, Chase's manifold articles (most of which featured in numerous editions of *The Campbellian*) on the estates' flora and fauna were consolidated in 1949 into *The Natural History of Campbell College and Cabin Hill*. He encouraged others – particularly pupils – to become engaged in the gathering of information. William MacQuitty – who left Campell in 1923, and later produced the film *A Night to Remember* – indicates in his autobiography (*A Life to Remember*) that he discovered a specimen of early purple orchid.

Others owed a greater debt to the idiosyncratic supernumerary schoolmaster. John Pate, a pupil at Campbell College in the late 1940s who lived in Cherryvalley, demonstrated an interest in birds. Chase fostered this enthusiasm, to the point of encouraging the young day-pupil to defy the school regulations and (along with boarding pupils) visit his first-floor room in the evenings by climbing a drain pipe and parapet. The illicit sessions paid dividends and Pate was later to acknowledge his debt, and he became successively Professor of Plant Physiology at QUB (1970) and Professor of Botany at the University of Western Australia (1974); like Chase's nephew (White), he was appointed a Fellow of the Australian Academy of Science (1980), and a Fellow of the Royal Society five years later.

The 'Chips' Factor

In 1958 Campbell College named a House in honour of Corrie Chase. He suffered illness in his final years, and spent some time in

Wandsworth Nursing Home, and finally at 51 Dundela Avenue, being cared for by Hanna MacMullan, but his name was closely linked with Campbell College until his death on 15 October 1965. His funeral service was held at Belmont Presbyterian Church where, despite being raised in the Anglican tradition, he had worshipped during his years at Campbell and where his name features on the congregational War Memorial. Following the service, the cortège then drove to the Belmont estate and wound through the grounds with which Chase had been so familiar, with the entire College lining the route in silent tribute. His remains were then taken to Roselawn Crematorium.

His sixty-year association resulted in inevitable comparisons with 'Mr Chips'. Chase fitted the legendary image in appearance, demeanour and disposition. He remained popular with pupils until his final days at the school, and was renowned for knowing all of them by name and being familiar with their genealogical ties for up to three generations. One early pupil, Dr Leslie Gregg (who was to become an expert in tropical diseases), wrote in tribute on Chase's death that: "I had the greatest regard for Mr Chase who appears to have become a real Mr Chips; he most certainly won my affection ... I cherish the memory of happy school days epitomised by C D Chase". Professor Pate echoed this sentiment: "A truly Mr Chips character in appearance and generosity of spirit if ever there was one".

The 'Chips' persona concealed one truly remarkable coincidence which no-one at the time – probably not even 'Chevy' Chase himself – realised. The Classics teacher whom Chase succeeded at Woodbridge School in 1900, and with whom he probably shook hands, was William H Balgarnie on his way to The Leys in Cambridge – where he matured into the very model for James Hilton's *Goodbye, Mr Chips!*

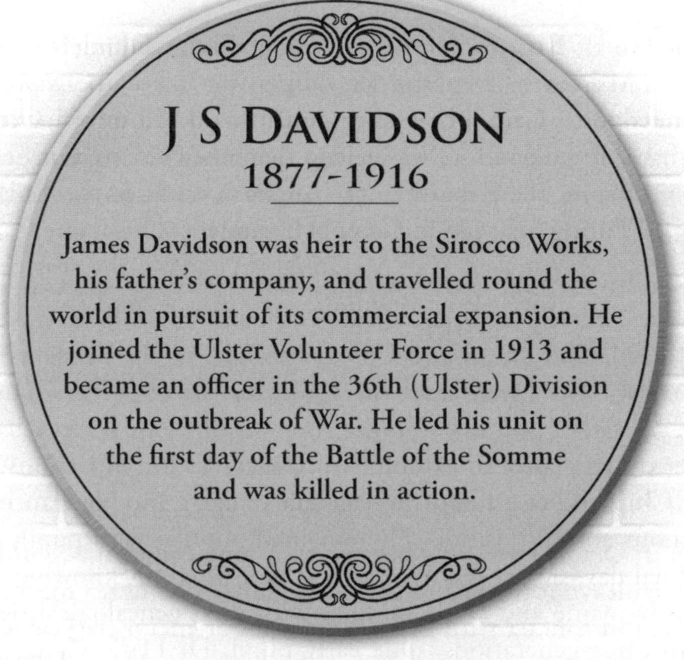

The Davidson family was rooted – almost literally – in East Belfast. Samuel Cleland Davidson, the great pioneering engineer who founded the Sirocco Works in 1881, established his name by streamlining the tea industry in India. He was born at the end of 1846 at Ballymaghan Farm, the eighth child of James, who owned 39 acres at Turf Lodge, at the junction of Holywood Arches. Samuel sired five children, of whom he outlived three; his elder son, James Samuel was born on 9 March 1877.

Heir to Sirocco

James and his younger brother, Richard (who died aged 18 in 1897) were educated at RBAI, where their father was a Governor, before being sent for a year to Paris. In September 1894 both sons enrolled at the newly opened Campbell College (for a year), primarily because it offered a Commercial training class. He then trained in his father's company at Bridge End, working initially in the Tea Machinery Department. Displaying "a keen perception of business possibilities", he was responsible for the introduction of Mechanical Stokers for Tea Drying machines, taking out patents for improving the department's hardware, such as the Enclosed Type of Tilting Tray Drier and Leaf Spreader!

Sirocco became an international business, partly as a consequence of James's travels on behalf of the company. In 1898 he travelled, via the Mediterranean and Constantinople, to the Russian Black Sea coast, Asia Minor and the Caucasus. In 1904, in company with his father and his younger sister (Kathleen), he travelled to America, primarily to exhibit Sirocco fans at the St Louis World Trade Fair and to attempt to establish an agency in New York.

Then in October 1910 he began a year long round-the-world trip in an endeavour to expand the firm's global sales of tea machinery. He kept in contact with Belfast by means of enciphered cable. For all the venture's apparent glamour of luxurious liners and the finest hotels, he endured many discomforts. The first stage of his journey to Bombay on board the H&W-built *SS Marmora* inspired complaints about cramped cabins! Headaches plagued him all his life, and were not eased by the humidity of Calcutta and Colombo (where Sirocco had opened a branch in 1892), from where he wrote to his mother that "The very effort of dressing is enough to make you feel as if you have been in a Turkish bath". He enjoyed memorable sights such as the Parsee Towers of Silence, the Himalayas and the Taj Mahal, but despised "the universal custom of trying to swindle you in everything you purchase".

He travelled to Penang, Singapore, Java and Hong Kong, and recorded that he was engaged almost daily in promoting and selling the company's new rollers, drying machinery and spare parts. The one disappointment was Japan where, he argued, the green tea "makes about as nasty a drink as you can imagine", and recognised that it offered few commercial opportunities. He crossed the Pacific to San Francisco via Hawaii; having been deprecating towards the oriental disposition, he balanced it with censure of western manners; he recorded that "A great many of the passengers [crossing the Pacific] are Americans of the pushing objectionable type who think everything belongs to them"! In Detroit he visited the American Blower Co, who held a Sirocco franchise, before returning to Belfast on 3 July 1911.

Despite being General Manager of, and heir to, what was probably the largest engineering business in the world, five years later, almost to the day, his body lay on the Somme battlefield amongst the carnage of the worst day in British military history.

36th (Ulster) Division

James Davidson was a sociable and popular individual who took full advantage of the opportunities which wealth offered (he left £21,929 2s 11d in his will). He was a member of the Ulster Club, the Ulster Reform Club, the Royal North of Ireland Yacht Club and the Royal Ulster Yacht Club where he sailed his Class III yacht, *Iris*. He became engaged to Eileen Rogers, a neighbour at Seacourt in Bangor. In an age where cars were a relative rarity, he owned two – a two-seater Delage which he bequeathed to his sister, and a four-seater Arrol Johnston, which he left to his business partner and fellow Battalion officer, Gerard Matthew.

With the formation of the UVF in early 1913, Matthew became a Company Commander in Newcastle. Davidson became an energetic member of 1 Battalion North Down Regiment in Bangor, of which his brother-in-law, Frederick Maguire, was second-in-command. With the formation of 36 (Ulster) Division in September 1914, all three men enlisted and Davidson earned a commission as a lieutenant on 18 September 1914, rising to the rank of captain in May 1915.

Many Co Down volunteers were attached to 13 Battalion Royal Irish Rifles in 108 Brigade, and in mid-September found themselves camped for training on Clandeboye estate. For all the recorded *esprit de corps*, there were 1300 men in the battalion and this presented considerable logistical problems, particularly with regard to culinary matters; Davidson and Matthew donated "a chimney and iron cooking plates to the cook house [and] also a large boiler for soup, etc".

His practical engineering skills brought him command of the battalion's machine-gun section, and in 1915 he passed two machine-gun courses for the Vickers and Lewis guns, and gained a 'distinction' in musketry training at Dollymount in Dublin. At the end of that year he was transferred to Seaford on the south coast of England where he was appointed Brigade Transport Officer. On 3 October 1915 his unit was despatched as part of the divisional advance party which embarked at Southampton. With a degree of irony, they travelled on board *SS Californian*, the captain of which, three years earlier, was pilloried for failing to assist the *Titanic*! It is likely to have occurred to Davidson that, like nearly all ships in the American, German and British navies, the vessel was equipped with ventilation equipment built by Sirocco!

The Somme

His first of ten billets in three months in France was a dilapidated château, where the conditions were little better than any of the trenches. He asked his mother to order plum puddings from Edinburgh and she forwarded "an occasional parcel of tinned things like galantine of chicken, sardines, etc. Kippered herrings and sausages (Palethorpes) also carry very well", he noted. His family correspondence reveals that, like most officers, he took advantage of his private income to cling to civilised bourgeois assurance and identity. Officers ordered bespoke tailoring and at the close of 1915 Davidson put a new pair of boots on his account at Manfield.

It was random fortune as to whether such luxuries were ever enjoyed. At the end of February 1916 he noted the perils of the German air force: "I have had a very close escape today … when suddenly there was a most extraordinary noise from somewhere above rather like an express train … and then came a terrific explosion about ten yards away". His last communication with home was penned at the height of the week-long bombardment of German lines preceding the Somme attack on 1 July 1916. On 28 June he wrote from Martinsart: "the din is awful now and it is almost impossible to think … Weather perfectly awful, torrents of rain". He asked his family to give his fiancée any personal items she may have wanted. Three days later the red and pale horsemen of the Apocalypse rode up for James Davidson, as they did for over 5000 other Ulstermen.

On that sunny but fateful morning he was ordered out of his reserve position at 8.10. Two hours he reported: "Am in B Line … We cannot possibly advance and reinforcements, ammunition and bombs are urgently needed". At 12.40 pm he reported a desperate situation: "I am holding the end of a communication trench with a Lewis gun. We cannot hold much longer. We are being pressed on all sides and ammunition almost finished". The War Diary of 13 Royal Irish Rifles noted that a runner "came in from the sunken road and reported Capt Davidson had been wounded in the knee and while [the runner] and another man were carrying him out he was shot dead between them".

Along with the inevitable royal telegram, Samuel Davidson received many messages of sympathy. One of James's fellow officers in the Machine-gun Company indicated that his colleague had been greatly respected both as an individual and an officer, and rehearsed the tragic events: "When things went badly, and he no doubt felt his obvious duty was to take up reinforcements, off he went, and for a long time he held up more or less single-handed a dangerous position; although shot through the knee, he refused to be carried back; alternately he fired his gun, and threw bombs until he had to retire to bind up his wound; he returned and did what he could, and finally he started back to try and find reinforcements. He was shortly after shot through the head". Capt Wilfrid Spender, who had formed the UVF, wrote with a degree of exaggeration from the Ulster Division HQ: "I am told your son fell after gallantry which deserved the VC ... The Division has covered itself in glory, which I don't think could be equalled by any other in the history of the world, if all the facts were known. An almost impossible task was set, and the Ulster Division did it".

Memorials

James Davidson's name was placed on the War Memorials of RBAI and Campbell College and at Bangor, and in a number of churches, and a plaque was erected to his memory in the Sirocco Works. He was one of fourteen pupils of Campbell College killed on 1 July 1916 and, along with the others who could not be identified, his name was placed on the massive Thiepval Memorial to the Missing. Unexpectedly, his body was later identified and was buried in plot XXX.E.7 of Serre Road no.2 Cemetery. His father died in 1921 and was buried in the City Cemetery and James's name was inscribed on the headstone.

R F Davis

1866-1937

Born and educated in Nottingham, Roby Davis studied at Cambridge and became a highly-respected Classics teacher in East Belfast where he lived. He was no stuffed shirt; he skated on Netherleigh lake, once crashing through the ice. He occasionally translated modern poetry into Greek and Latin, and one of his verses found its way into the English Hymnal. His death was recorded in *The Times*.

Robert – often known more affectionately as Roby – Davis was born in Nottingham on 22 January 1866, the son of Charlotte (née Furley) and Robert Davis, a lace warehouseman. Despite this apparently humble social background, he performed well academically at Nottingham High School and matriculated as a Scholar at St John's College, Cambridge, at Michaelmas 1885, earning a First Class degree in the Classical Tripos three years later.

He arrived in Belfast in September 1902 from Leamington College to become Senior Classical Master at Campbell College. Only a few years earlier he might have been dissuaded from this career move by his exact contemporary, Henry Joseph Spenser. The two men were born in the same year, both attending Nottingham High School and St John's College contemporaneously. Spenser had been one of the original staff at Campbell College when it opened on 3 September 1894, but he became a victim of a bitter and public dispute between the Headmaster and Staff, which became a cause célèbre in the Dublin courts, the consequences of which almost caused the school to close its doors within two years. Spenser departed – effectively dismissed – in the summer of 1896, but became a successful Headmaster at schools in England and, by coincidence, died in the same year as Davis. (One of Davis' early pupils at Belmont from 1903 – Elliott Johnston (see separate entry) – had coincidentally previously been educated at Nottingham High School).

Classics Teacher

Robert Davis's interest in the Classics post at Campbell may have owed something to the fact that his predecessor, Robert Knox McElderry, had emulated his First Class degree in Classics at the same Cambridge College in 1896 and may during his studies have read recent publications bearing McElderry's name. McElderry, who became Professor of Greek at Galway (1902-1924) and at QUB (1924-1934), could have proved a hard act to follow, but the Englishman's reputation as a Classics teacher was to prove formidable and enduring.

In 1894 he edited a volume of Tacitus's *Germania* (including an introduction and notes), and in the following year jointly produced a translation of *The Hymns of Prudentius*. In 1906 one of the latter was adopted as one of two versions in the English Hymnal (no.613) of the Christmas procession *Of the Father's Love Begotten*, which has also featured in subsequent hymnals such as *Rejoice in the Lord* (hymn no.191). During the early days of his Campbell career – for his own amusement and that of his pupils – the Cambridge scholar would also translate into Greek and Latin extracts from Tennyson, Longfellow and even W S Gilbert.

In 1944 one anonymous former pupil claimed that Davis was "debonair, humorous, rich in personality and entertainments, who would go to any pains to do the slightest service for a boy in need"; and his most celebrated pupil, E R Dodds, reflected on the recognition of his older students of "how much genuine kindness lay behind his deliberately dry manner". Harry Cronne, who arrived at Campbell College from Portaferry in 1917 and later became a Professor of Medieval History, believed that the Classics scholar "exercised a much-needed civilising influence in the school" and compared his teaching to "soft rain after a prolonged drought".

Davis was well-respected despite his short stature; Dodds recalled that he was "a tiny man who wielded the quiet authority of a true scholar", echoed in the sentiment that Davis possessed "a small, trim personage, with beautiful hands and beautiful manners". There were occasions when his equanimity and ready good humour served him well. Clarke MacDermott, later to become Lord Chief Justice of Northern Ireland, recalled that when he was a pupil at Campbell College it was not uncommon during harsh winters for locals to skate on the frozen lake at Netherleigh. He revealed that Davis "skated gracefully and partnered his wife, a tall and athletic lady [Greta Keenleyside, whom he had married in Nottingham], and his performance certainly lost no marks with his juvenile audience; but I doubt if in the end it added much to his rating, as one afternoon they both went through a thin spot together, she up to her knees, he nearer his midriff, and patently in greater need of succour than his spouse". Davis's athletic instinct is echoed in membership of Strandtown Lawn Tennis & Croquet Club, and of Holywood Golf Club.

He was popularly known amongst the pupils at Belmont as 'Pussy' Davis, a nickname which derived from the feline aspect he projected via his moustache with stiffly-waxed points, sleek hair, oval pince-nez and purring voice. A pupil from the first decade of the 20th century recalled the school's horse-drawn lawnmower "whose gentle whirring sound drifted up from the cricket fields in summer and mingled with the dry, crisp tones of Pussy Davis taking us through some Sophoclean text". The Classics teacher was to be incapacitated for the whole of the Christmas term of 1919 as a result of contracting influenza, and it may have been as a consequence of this infection that he lost the use of an eye.

As in most other educational establishments of the age, there was regular recourse to the cane – and, indeed, some other more esoteric methods of discipline. One colleague at Campbell College – who acquired, for unknown reasons, the nickname of 'Bubbles' – "required offenders to put on a lady's high-heeled, lace-up boots and parade up and down his study"! Roby Davis exercised greater subtlety. Clarke MacDermott considered that he "was not only a fine scholar but an excellent teacher [of Latin and Greek] ... He took pains with the dull as well as the bright, and his incisive manner and capacity as a disciplinarian, who seldom needed to raise his voice, gave every chance to those in his classes; but he enjoyed teaching the keen boys and was very successful with them". Eric Dodds – who derived a certain pride from having been expelled from Campbell in 1912 for, as he expressed it, "gross, studied and sustained insolence to the Headmaster" – was to become Regius Professor of Greek at Oxford University (1936-1960), and he acknowledged his academic and intellectual debt to Davis, who offered "a perfect lesson in the technique and the good manners of controversy – how to use the rapier against the bludgeon and how to kill a bad argument mercifully". Like his colleague Lewis Alden (see separate entry), he exhorted a wide range of reading, and encouraged pupils (in Dodds's words) "to read ancient [Classical] authors rapidly and in bulk for the matter as well as the language".

Extra-curricular

Roby Davis played an active role in the extra-curricular life of Campbell College. He was a competent violinist, and gave solo performances at the school's Hallowe'en concerts between 1902 and 1907. He also contributed – as did his wife – to the production of all school plays. He proved a sociable colleague, and one of his pupils and later colleague, Kenneth Armour [youngest of three sons of Rev J B Armour, Presbyterian Home Rule minister of Ballymoney] – who also followed Davis as a graduate in Classics at Cambridge – cherished the memory of him as "a man whose being was almost wholly composed of sympathy and cheerfulness ... standing in the Common Room, his back to the fire, an ancient pipe in his hand, full of animated talk on any variety of subjects". Armour continued: "He was one of those rare people whose frank criticism is more to be valued than most men's praise, intolerant only of the casual and the bigot".

As Eric Dodds noted in his personal tribute to Davis, the schoolmaster was conservative in his political views. At the time of the seminal National Insurance Act of 1911 he composed a poem (entitled *The School Insurance Bill*) in which he appears to mock its aspirations as undermining personal responsibility. In September 1912 he supported the imperialist ethos of the College by standing in line with 100 others – in the College itself – to sign the Solemn League & Covenant against the introduction of Home Rule in Ireland. As an Englishman, he could have argued that it was not his political struggle, but – in addition to the Omagh-born Headmaster – six other members of Staff appended their signature, only one of whom was of Irish birth!

The inter-War policy of the Governors of Campbell College required members of Staff to retire at the age of sixty. Davis's talents were sufficiently respected, however, for them to allow him an extension of four years, and he eventually retired in the summer of 1931. In contrast to the majority of his colleagues, the fact that he was married obliged him to live outside the school. His first address was 4 Kincora Avenue which, until approximately 1907, was originally listed as Belmont Park. The house was initially named Penrith Villa, but Davis changed its name to Rodven. The nomenclature clearly had some personal resonance as, when he moved around February 1920 to 31 Wandsworth Road, which was originally known as Springvale, he also rechristened it as Rodven.

On 26 October 1908 he made a simple will – leaving everything he owned to his wife – on a single page of foolscap paper, which was witnessed by two Campbell College colleagues, Raywood Beaven and George Thompson. When he died without issue at Rodven on 14 February 1937 his gross assets totalled £246 2s 7d – probably a reflection of the fact that, between the Wars, schoolteaching was a very poorly-rewarded profession. His wife's name is given as Elizabeth Ann, and it is unclear whether 'Greta' was an affectionate name bestowed upon her, or whether at some stage Davis had remarried. His wife lived on in Wandsworth Road until approximately 1943. Although there was no full obituary, his passing was listed in the death notices of The Times.

E J HARLAND
1831-1895

A Yorkshireman by birth, Edward Harland quickly purchased a ship-building interest in Belfast in the 1850s, and subsequently established the largest ship-building yards in the world. As well as being a businessman, he was a pioneer of ship design, which helped to keep him ahead of his competitors. He later became Harbour Commissioner, Mayor of Belfast and a Belfast MP.

Edward Harland was one of those single-minded individuals who, in company with such as Samuel Davidson and William Holmes Smiles (see separate entry), established a business in East Belfast which was counted amongst the largest of its kind in the world.

Apprentice

The only thing which the author of this volume has in common with Harland is that we were both born in Scarborough. His father was a doctor with a penchant for mechanical pursuits, and was familiar with the locomotive engineer, George Stephenson, with whose family's engineering firm Edward was provided with a five-year apprenticeship on his fifteenth birthday. One year was spent in the drawing office, and it is claimed that his professional determination was strengthened as a result of failing to win first prize for a new lifeboat design. He found the entire period arduous but rewarding: "I was now in my element", he later recalled, "The working hours were very long … from six in the morning until 6.15 at night, except Saturday (which was 4 pm)". An obituary in *The Northern Whig* claimed: "He cared during this time of his career very little for his personal comfort, or even for the not very agreeable effluvia of the river [Tyne]. He had not, he said, suffered from the stench; he did not see therefore why others should consider it a nuisance. During those years … he had to content himself often with somewhat hard fare. He had not long ago talked of the days when he went to work with a herring for breakfast in his pocket".

Belfast

At the close of his apprenticeship a considerable economic recession was in progress, but he took the opportunity to visit, and be inspired by, the Great Exhibition (1851). His professional opening came as a consequence of the fact that one of his relatives was married to German merchant and financier, Gustav Schwabe (based in Liverpool), who was also the uncle of his future partner, Gustav Wolff. Schwabe provided the ambitious Yorkshireman with introductions and over the next three years the young engineer displayed considerable talent at shipyards and marine engineers in Glasgow and on the Tyne, where he rapidly "recognised the great importance of quality control in achieving commercial success, and he would not tolerate poor workmanship". This attitude was echoed in memories of him at his own future shipyard where "a bit of chalk was ever in his vest pocket; he made a white circle around any defect he would see in the workshops of the ships for earliest attention. Another constant companion was an ivory foot rule".

With only three years of practical experience he was offered in 1854 the position of manager at the shipyard of Robert Hickson

& Co in Belfast, established on the recently-created Queen's Island (in which Gustav Wolff was also employed). Harland quickly identified production failings in the yard and brought across trusted workers from England and recruited Wolff as his assistant. Very soon "new orders were forthcoming for several large sailing ships and screw propelled ships".

Harland purchased Hickson's yard in 1858 with financial assistance from Schwabe, who was partner in John Bibby Sons & Co, which placed an order for three screw propelled steamships. The expanding order book resulted in Harland taking on Wolff as a partner and forming the world-renowned company in 1861.

Inventor

Other local businessmen have tended to outshine Harland as pioneers – Samuel Davidson, for instance, is credited with 120 patents. Nevertheless, as *The Daily Star* wrote in its tribute to the shipbuilder "He was not merely a highly competent businessman; he is entitled to take his place amongst the great innovators of the last half of the [19th] century. The long and narrow vessels, which we now know … as ocean greyhounds, were of his design". Harland began to design ships with greater length to accommodate increased tonnage and with a flat bottom; he also built the upper deck entirely of iron. Sceptics and competitors christened them 'Bibby coffins'; they did, however, cut eight days off the trans-Atlantic crossing.

The Northern Whig's edition on Christmas Day 1895 (the morning after his death) encapsulated his talent: "His inventive ability and technical skill were also judiciously employed, particularly in connection with special classes of ships for special trades. The long, narrow, flat-sided almost flat-bottomed cargo ship, which is the only type of ocean steamer that can be made to pay under modern conditions, owes its origin to his remarkable combination of business shrewdness and constructive genius". In 1871 Harland had taken out a patent for a new propeller arrangement, and the magazine *The Rialto* concluded that his "greatest achievement is the twin screw, and this made the name of the firm".

In 1868 Schwabe helped Thomas Henry Ismay of Liverpool to purchase the White Star Line (which was eventually transformed into the Oceanic Steam Navigation Company), and the resultant expanding order book necessitated the modernisation and expansion of the shipyard. The *Oceanic* in 1871 was the first of many ships constructed for the Company. In 1889 two further ships named *Teutonic* and *Majestic* were built for the White Star Line. It has been claimed that the former was named in honour of the Germanic Wolff, whilst the second honoured Harland, reflecting comments made about his ramrod gait and demeanour, as represented in his statue at Belfast City Hall.

Two other partners were eventually taken on: William (later Viscount) Pirrie, who was very successful in maintaining a full order book, and Walter Wilson, who was primarily responsible for the development of the cabin accommodation as trans-Atlantic competition intensified (although, as can be seen in the entry for James Davidson, complaints were not unknown!) Although Wilson and Wolff never got married, both Pirrie and Harland did so – but it is an odd coincidence that not one of the four partners produced any offspring!

Later Years

Harland (like Pirrie) was a disciplinarian, but a fair employer and, although he opposed Home Rule, he was equally hostile to the sectarianism which was to plague Harland & Wolff. In the mid-1870s he began to reduce his commitment to the shipyard, and ceased to be a partner in 1884. Between 1874 and 1886 he acted as Chairman of the Belfast Harbour Commissioners. He was Mayor of Belfast in 1885 and 1886, welcoming the Prince and Princess of

Wales during their Irish tour; he was rewarded with a knighthood which was promoted to a baronetcy during his second year of office. He represented North Belfast at Westminster between 1889 and his death.

He had lived in earlier days in North Belfast, but later occupied Edenvale in Strandtown before moving further along the Belmont Road to Ormiston. He died suddenly late on Christmas Eve 1895 at Glenfarne Castle (not Glengorme, as is stated in *The Dictionary of Irish Biography*) which he rented in Co Leitrim. According to the Irish press, he seems to have expressed some wish to be laid to rest in Brompton Churchyard near Scarborough, where his parents were buried. His wife, Rosa Wann, who had lived at Wilmont (now in Sir Thomas and Lady Dixon Park; not Vermont, as some sources claim) came from Belfast, however, and it may have been out of respect for her wishes that he was buried in Belfast City Cemetery.

T JACKSON
1807-1890

Visionary architect Thomas Jackson was a Waterford Quaker who settled in Belfast and, in conjunction with Sir Thomas McClure, was responsible for the design and development of many of the villas and mansions in East Belfast such as Glenmachan. He was related to the prolific local Greeves family. His son designed the Old Town Hall in Belfast.

The architect Thomas Jackson appears to have operated a mutually-beneficial partnership with the local land-owner at Belmont, Thomas McClure. Jackson's pen and set-square provided the materialisation of McClure's vision for the district, the means by which those who leased McClure's estates fulfilled their contractual obligation to construct a permanent and suitable residence. Indeed, Jackson initiated the building of villas in the area when he entered into an arrangement with McClure on 7 June 1860 (on a 10,000 year lease) for the development of the land "on the east side of the Old Holywood Road", which is now Glenmachan Road.

One commentator has observed of Jackson that his "principal contribution to Belfast ... was his attempt to improve the standard of suburban development" and he was committed to the aesthetic blending of the properties in the locality, which one architectural historian dubbed 'Jacksonville'. He had made an initial attempt at such a philosophy in the early 1840s with the promotion of Cliftonville (probably named after the area of Bristol where he had studied) in North Belfast. By 1861 he was advertising – effectively as an agent for McClure – villa sites "in the immediate vicinity of picturesque and romantic glens and walks" in the locality.

Jackson himself laid the foundations of the area's development around 1860 by building a residence for himself called Glenmachan. This was promptly purchased by Sir William Ewart, probably as a ready-made means of fulfilling his obligation to McClure. As a replacement for Glenmachan, in 1864 Jackson designed Altona a short distance away – which has remained in the hands of his family and descendants down to the present day. Set in eight and a half acres – of which, towards the end of his life, he acquired the freehold – Altona was described by one source as "a model of convenience combined with that characteristic restraint which sets Jackson's work aside from that of the majority of mid-Victorian architects ... it was just a small part of a grand design for developing the Sydenham hillside with a series of ... really big wooded gardens for successful industrialists".

Quakers

Thomas Jackson was born on 31 August 1807 to Quaker parents in Waterford, where the Society of Friends was at the commercial and industrial heart of the coastal city. His father, Anthony, was a Freeman of that city and in accordance with the strictest Quaker ordinances – not to marry out of the Society – Anthony married Elizabeth Pim from Cork. Two of their sons – Thomas and John Pim Jackson – both eventually became architects in Belfast, but a personal and professional association with the south coast was maintained as, on 1 January 1835, Thomas Jackson married Lydia Newsom Ridgway of Waterford. Thomas's will reveals that he continued to hold property on the quayside at Waterford which he inherited from his father-in-law.

Thomas Jackson was a devoted family man whose lengthy will made provision for his children and grand-children, plus the families of his siblings, to whom he demonstrated much more affection than did his Belmont neighbour, Joseph Malcomson Greeves of Bernagh on Circular Road, towards his own. This could have proved an awkward relationship for Jackson – for Greeves was his grandson. Greeves's father, John, had married Elizabeth Pim Jackson. Like his wife, he came from solid Quaker stock but at some stage moved to the harsher branch of the Brethren which was to leave its mark on Joseph, who was described by C S Lewis as "severe in his dress and in his expression ... the face ... at once oppressed and oppressive". His characterisation as "a harsh husband and a despotic father", who often reduced his wife (an American) to tears, contrasted with the architect's obvious affection for "my dear wife".

Whether Thomas Jackson was ever dismayed by such circumstances does not appear to be recorded, but he evidently did not harbour any resentment about the course of the life which his daughter adopted, as he left all four of his daughters an equal share of the benefits accruing from various shares and bonds. He also left Joseph's first-born son, who was born only two years before Thomas Jackson's own death, the not-insubstantial sum of £100; he was probably greatly touched that the child (his great-grandson) – who later became an Irish rugby international between 1907 and 1909 and President of Irish Rugby Football Union in 1929 – had been christened Thomas Jackson Greeves!

Elizabeth Jackson's elder sister, Georgina Eliza Jackson, married her brother-in-law's brother, Thomas Malcomson Greeves, and the latter and his brother (John) formed J & TM Greeves, Flax Spinners, whose Mills were designed by their father-in-law. Perhaps inevitably, Thomas Jackson also designed their family homes close to his own. Tweskard was built for Thomas Malcomson, and (in 1869) Lismachan, at the end of Glenmachan Road, was built for John; three years later the latter was adorned by a gate-lodge designed by Jackson's elder son, Anthony Thomas, whose principal, but not entirely appreciated, work was the Old Town Hall in Victoria Street, Belfast, in 1871.

Such residences illustrate that, for all their more severe approach to life and their austere form of worship, the Greeves family were not averse to enjoying the benefits of their prosperity. As he distributed his wealth amongst his own family, Thomas Jackson acknowledged that he had been "blessed ... by a Kind Providence". He invested in bonds and securities at home and overseas; he was averse, however, to risky ventures. His will evinces irritation at "a Skating Rink Speculation on which I had not been consulted" undertaken in 1878 by his younger son, William Ridgway Jackson (who died in Australia in 1886), and he appears to have made provision for his widowed daughter-in-law to finance £1521 owed to the Ulster Bank.

As Altona was never offered for sale, it is difficult to determine how lavishly – or otherwise – Thomas Jackson furnished his home, but he had a great fondness for his book collection, which featured 800 volumes embossed with initials and a family bible which had belonged to his grandfather (also named Thomas). Although common-place as a contemporary means of family record, there is perhaps a touch of vanity in the portraits he commissioned of himself and his wife by Richard Hooke, who had painted portraits of five Mayors of Belfast in addition to an Archbishop of Armagh. Perhaps the most surprising items in a Quaker will – although it may have been a conventional phrase in the wills of most businessmen – were the 'wines and liquors' which he left with the rest of his domestic items to his younger daughter, Gilbertina Newsom Jackson.

Architect

Thomas Jackson was articled to George Dymond, a Quaker architect based in Bristol. He arrived in Belfast in 1829 to run the new Waring Street office of his partner, Thomas Duff of Newry. He worked on commissions for Hans Blackwood of Killyleagh and the Marquess of Dufferin & Ava (also of the Blackwood family) on the Clandeboye estate. His principal work in these early years (c.1830-1831) was what is now referred to as the Old Museum (still extant) in College Square North, designed in the neo-Classical style.

Probably as a consequence of his marriage at the very start of 1835 and of a desire to pursue a more personal and creative approach to his portfolio, he terminated the partnership with Duff and formed his own practice (based in the same Waring Street office). At the same time, influenced by the garden suburb of Clifton which he had seen in Bristol he purchased land as a speculative venture in North Belfast, once known as Solitude but which he named Cliftonville. The fundamental vision was "of comfortable villas set in generously scaled gardens and joined by tree-lined streets". It proved to be a commercial failure, although he retained the land and property.

One of his early major projects in Belfast town centre was St Malachy's Church (1840-1844) in Alfred Street. Designed in the Tudor Gothic style and described by one commentator as "a superb example of Sir-Walter-Scottery at its most romantic", it demonstrated that he was not inhibited by any religious scruples which might have demanded conformity to his own more simplistic form of worship and meeting place. During half a century of output, he was to tackle a variety of work: as well as commercial properties (which included work on nineteen Ulster Bank premises), he accepted industrial, educational and ecclesiastical contracts, in addition to the diverse domestic residences. The few villas attributed to him in South Belfast appear to be unexceptional Victorian two-storey homes, such as Tighnabruaich in Derryvolgie Avenue. This had been built in 1880 for the Dixon family but, following a bankruptcy order, Jackson acquired it on 28 October 1881 as the residence of his son (Anthony Thomas).

In contrast, a number of the houses which he designed in the Belmont area were Italianate in style, including Glenmachan Tower which was built in the early 1860s for Thomas McClure and Schomberg which was occupied by Sir William Quartus Ewart (the son of the owner of Glenmachan) – both of which have since been demolished – and Craigavon, built in 1870 for James Craig, but now in a seriously dilapidated condition.

Death

Thomas Jackson, having just celebrated his 83rd birthday, died at Altona on 3 September 1890, having contracted two days earlier "a severe illness terminating in death by apoplexy". He was buried alongside his wife (died 28 January 1879) and his youngest brother (died 18 June 1847) in the Friends' Burial Ground at Balmoral. Altona and its contents were left to his unmarried daughter, Gilbertina Newsom Jackson, "who has been my constant companion and housekeeper" since her mother died. Gilbertina died (aged 76) on 16 May 1920; however, as early as 1900 Altona had also become the residence of Arthur, a brother of John Greeves (the convert to the Brethren). Arthur's son, John Ronald Howard, was born there in 1900 and lived in the house – which remains one of the oldest habitations in Belmont – until his death in 1988.

E JOHNSTON
1888-1916

Elliott Johnston worked for his father's company in Newtownards, although the family resided in East Belfast. He became actively involved in the Ulster Volunteer Force and was subsequently an officer in the 36th (Ulster) Division. He was decorated for his courage in the trenches, but was killed on the opening day of the Battle of the Somme.

Elliott Johnston, who was given his mother's maiden name, was born on 12 May 1888 at Hartford Lodge in Newtownards, the second son of Samuel Johnston, Managing Director of the Glen Printing & Finishing Works. Elliott was first educated at Nottingham High School, where Robert Furley Davis (see separate entry), one of his later teachers at Campbell College, had also been taught. By the time he arrived at Campbell in September 1903, Elliott's family was resident at Ardenza (still extant) on the King's Road at Knock.

Elliott attended QUB before being employed, as one source states, as a Linen Manufacturer's Manager, which in reality meant being engaged by his father as Manager of the hemstitching department (and as a Director) at the Glen Works. Whilst at QUB he had served two years in the newly-formed OTC, which provided him with military training which ultimately singled him out as a Half-

Company Commander in 'D' Company of 2 Battalion (North Down Regiment) of the Newtownards UVF between 1913 and 1914.

When war broke out in Europe, Elliott was granted a Temporary Commission on 29 September 1914, and trained at the Clandeboye estate with 13 Battalion (Co Down Volunteers) Royal Irish Rifles of 108 Brigade in 36 (Ulster) Division. He rose to the rank of Lieut in December 1914, obtained a 1st Class Instructor's badge at the Dollymount School of Musketry and, by the time of the departure of the Division in the summer of 1915, the men of Newtownards were placed under the command of joint-Adjutants of the battalion: Elliott Johnston and Lieut William Martin Wright. The latter was one of six sons – all of whom fought in the First World War – of Rev Dr William Martin, who had been Presbyterian minister in Newtownards since 1879 and was chaplain of the local UVF. On 24 June 1915 the staff and employees of the Glen Works presented a gift to their popular Manager, which included a combination knife, fork and spoon, a clasp knife, map case, prismatic compass, an inscribed watch with luminous dial, and a service revolver. The presentation included the prophetic observation that, amongst the men of Newtownards, "all might not be spared to come back".

Military Cross

In February 1916 Elliott Johnston was raised to the rank of Captain. At only 147 lbs, yet one inch short of six feet tall, he was a spare but impressive figure, and demonstrated promising leadership qualities. On the night of 26 June 1916 he organised and led a raid of one hundred men on enemy support trenches, reaching the most advanced position attained at that stage of the conflict, capturing a German officer and twelve soldiers. Colonel W H Savage of 13 Battalion Royal Irish Rifles described this to Samuel Johnston as "the most successful raid done by our Division". Although personally congratulated by General Nugent, Elliott was never to read the announcement in The London Gazette on 26 September of the award to him of the MC. His father asked for the medal to be sent to Ardenza, but he eventually received it from Brig-General Hacket Pain, under whom his son had served in the UVF, at a ceremony at Palace Barracks in Holywood.

A telegram was sent from Buckingham Palace on 11 July 1916 to Ardenza, which confirmed that Elliott Johnston was one of almost 20,000 men (including 5500 Ulstermen) to be killed on 1 July, the opening day of the Battle of the Somme. On that morning he was in command of nos. 5 & 7 platoons in 'B' Company of 13 Battalion Royal Irish Rifles. Two of the soldiers who fought alongside him as they left the trenches in Thiepval Wood at 7.30 am later reported that the captain was shot about half-an-hour into the attack, as they approached the second line of the German trenches. A machine-gun bullet went through him just above the hip, and it proved impossible to offer him any assistance as "the enemy kept a machine-gun firing over the spot where he fell". It was, in any case, believed that he had died almost immediately. Elliott Johnston's body was never identified, and his name is recorded on Pier and Face 15A & 15B on the Thiepval Memorial. His name also features on the War Memorials at the North of Ireland Football Club, in Strandtown and Newtownards, and at Campbell College and QUB. In recent years his MC has been donated to the Somme Heritage Centre, not far from his original home.

Family

Colonel Savage, his Commanding Officer, wrote to Samuel Johnston when returning the officer's possessions: "It may be some pride to you to know that your son was held in the highest estimation in the battalion and, by his gallantry in the field, earned great credit for his old battalion". Samuel Johnston, whose wife had died in 1915, moved from Ardenza to Deramore Park off the Malone Road before purchasing, in 1930, Little Lea on Circular Road in Belmont from C S Lewis following the death of the latter's father.

Elliott's younger brother, Ernest Clifford Johnston, ran the Old Manor Mill – producing flour and feeding stuffs – on Mill Street in Newtownards, but was ultimately unable to compete with the larger integrated millers, and the business closed in 1937. The eldest son, William, was sent by his father in 1913 to run the Manchester base of the company operations. He volunteered his services to Fred Crawford and the UVF gun-runners, and during the next year smuggled three million rounds of .303 ammunition and 500 rifles into Ulster in bleaching powder barrels padded with farina. All three brothers served in the UVF, and readily stored some of the 25,000 rifles smuggled by Crawford either into Bangor or Donaghadee in April 1914 in the Glen Works, which finally closed its doors in 1932.

Elliott composed his will at Bordon Army Camp in Hampshire on 4 October 1915, immediately prior to leaving for France. He left sums of between £25 and £50 to Julia, Edith and Irene, his sisters; the latter was shortly to be married to a Canadian. He left the rest to a lady named 'Trixie' – adding that, if she were his wife by the time he died, she was to inherit everything. He estimated that she would receive approximately £825, but his effects totalled £2007 14 s 9d.

T G Kent
1911-1988

Tyler Kent was educated briefly in East Belfast. He later worked for the American Embassy in London where he intercepted secret intelligence and passed it to the Germans. He was arrested and imprisoned for treason. After the War he married a wealthy American heiress whom he eventually ruined financially.

As he stepped on to American soil on 4 December 1945, after five years' incarceration for treason, Tyler Gatewood Kent bore an uncanny resemblance to Ian Fleming, the creator of James Bond. It was entirely apposite, for both men were incorrigible womanisers, inveterately arrogant, inclined to pursue a life-style beyond their modest salary and were closely engaged in the world of espionage. There was much that could also be applied to Fleming (apart from the nationality) in a description of Kent offered by journalist and author Malcolm Muggeridge: "One of those intensely gentlemanly Americans who wear well-cut tailor-made suits, with waistcoat and watch-chain, drink wine instead of high-balls, and easily become furiously indignant".

Tyler Kent arrived at Belmont in 1920, aged nine, when his father was transferred to Belfast as a member of the American Consular Service. The family resided at Pine Lodge, now a residential home on the Belmont Road (opposite the entrance to Strathearn) and, although younger than most of his fellow pupils, young Tyler was educated at Campbell College, until he was despatched to Connecticut for his education in the summer of 1924. He was placed at Campbell at much the same age as had been C S Lewis a decade earlier and it would be interesting to know if they garnered similar impressions of the ethos of the school. (It is not beyond the bounds of possibility that the young man and boy passed on the street, as Lewis visited his family and friends at Belmont in December 1920 and September 1921, and Pine Lodge was en route from the Lewis home to that of his friends, the McNeills). In later life, however, their world view radically diverged. C S Lewis was moulded by the tradition of service to the Empire which prevailed in East Belfast, whilst Kent came to loathe everything British; as one source noted: "from the time of his arrival in England [1939] until his death on 20 November 1988, [Kent] never had a good word to say about the British, their system, or any single Briton". Nevertheless, although his later life convincingly demonstrated that he was not readily susceptible to sentimentality, he appears to have retained some affection for Campbell College because as late as 1938, whilst employed by the American Embassy in Moscow, he sent the Headmaster a Christmas card.

Kent – who was distantly related to American heroes General George Patton and Davy Crockett – was appointed a cipher clerk in 1934 in the newly opened Embassy in Moscow. During the next five years he proved to be an employee of dubious morality, engaged in shady dealings, and such a character continued to manifest itself when he was transferred to London in October 1939. Despite the fact that the Americans had their own suspicions about his activities, and the fact that within two days of his arrival in London he was placed under MI5 surveillance, his post at the Embassy involved coding and decoding and access to every signal which went through the system.

Despite being employed by the American Government, he was incensed by President Roosevelt's willingness (in contravention of his country's official neutrality) to offer Churchill secret support, by-passing Chamberlain, in the early days of the Second World War. He copied nearly 2000 cables which he channelled to German Intelligence via the conduit of the Italian Embassy in London. One interpretation suggests that Mussolini was induced by Hitler to remain neutral in late 1939 and early 1940 in order to keep open this invaluable source of information and that it was only after Kent was arrested on 20 May 1940 that Il Duce declared his support for Germany on 10 June 1940.

Kent was arrested at his home in Gloucester Court in London – ironically as he was receiving a telephone call from the Italian Embassy – in possession of over 1900 documents, which at his trial were described as "the whole confidential communication system of the United States". He was tried under the Official Secrets' Act and although he had hopes that he could be tried in an American court, where his actions might have been viewed more favourably, the American Ambassador, Joe Kennedy, waived Kent's diplomatic immunity – primarily because his own scorn for and ill-disposition towards the British had also been so embarrassingly disclosed. Having been found guilty, Kent spent five years incarcerated on the Isle of Wight before being deported to America after the end of the War.

A Trailer Park

In 1946 Kent facilitated the promulgation of his extremist views by marrying Clara Hyatt, a multi-millionairess whose fortune was provided by Carter's Little Liver Pills (probably the best marriage by a former Campbell College pupil since William Greeves, brother of CS Lewis's close friend, Arthur, had married the Cadbury heiress in 1918). In later life Clara may well have wished that she had force-fed large quantities of the pills to her excessively profligate husband who ran through her wealth with such reckless extravagance that they ended their days living in a trailer park.

The integral educational philosophy of the school at Belmont between the Wars had been a preparation for service in the British Empire. This clearly had no impact upon the young Tyler, who readily assisted the aspirations of Hitler's Reich. Ironically, it was to be the work of a fellow pupil, Eric Megaw (see separate entry) – who will have crossed the path of the American for six months in the corridors at Campbell – who did much to challenge the Führer's threat to Britain with his crucial development in 1940 (completed around the very time of Kent's arrest) of the cavity magnetron, used in radar. After the Second World War, his former school applied the 'Oscar Wilde principle' to Tyler Kent. Following his conviction for homosexuality, Portora expunged Wilde's name from its Honours' boards, although it was later restored. Campbell appears to have done likewise with the name of Tyler Kent in the occasional publication of its *Registers*.

Whilst he was at Campbell he will probably have had to sing the school song, with its antique Victorian philosophy. The final couplet romanticises that the world will say: "There goes a man that's neither rogue nor fool, Dead straight in all he says and does, true son of such a school". One wonders whether these words resonated with Tyler Gatewood Kent during his interrogation in 1940 when one of his inquisitors said: "I am afraid that I must take the view that you are either a fool or a rogue"!

R W LESLIE
1862-1931

Dr Richard Leslie was a well-known medical figure in East Belfast, and was particularly friendly with C S Lewis's father. He was popular and widely respected although his medical skills were occasionally lampooned, and he was known to the younger generation as 'Squeaky Dick'. He was a staunch and active Unionist during the years of the Home Rule Crisis.

History and record have left a variable memorial to this prominent member of the medical profession and East Belfast community. Born on 26 September 1862, Richard Whytock Leslie was the son of Rev John Knox Leslie, minister of 3rd Cookstown Presbyterian Church from November 1835. The family was to develop a prominent status within the Presbyterian fold, and his father died in May 1902 as Father of the General Assembly. In addition to his son, the clergyman also fathered two daughters who both married Presbyterian clergymen. The younger daughter (Margaret Barnett Leslie) married Rev William McKean, who was appointed Moderator of the General Assembly in 1906, in which position he was followed by his son, Rev John Knox Leslie McKean in 1952.

Richard Whytock Leslie was educated at Cookstown Academy and Raphoe Royal School before qualifying in medicine in 1887 at the

Royal University of Ireland in Galway and Belfast. He also became a licentiate in midwifery at the Rotunda Hospital in Dublin. In 1894 Dr Leslie was appointed physician to the Ulster Hospital for Children & Women (in Templemore Avenue, where he served until 1929) and also to Campbell College (where he stayed until two months before his death in September 1931). He resided for about two years at St Andrew's Terrace in Strandtown, before moving in 1894 to St Heliers on Belmont Road, where he lived until his death. His obituary in *The Northern Whig* described him as "one of the best-known medical practitioners in East Belfast for many years" and he was well-respected within his profession. He was an active member of the Ulster Medical Society, serving as President in 1912-1913, and of the provincial branch of the British Medical Association. (His many other related medical offices are detailed in his obituary in *The British Medical Journal*, 3 October 1931, p.635).

Over many years, as Medical Secretary of the Ulster Branch of the St John Ambulance Association, Dr Leslie devoted much time to running first-aid and ambulance classes, particularly in the Strandtown area. These were occasionally treated to a degree of raillery; in 1903 the Prefects"Log Book of Campbell College records: "An Ambulance Class was held. We may now get hurt as much as we like". On 21 March 1908 he gave a lecture, accompanied by a practical demonstration on a pupil, on the subject of 'The resuscitation of the apparently drowned'. His dedication was acknowledged with the appointment as a Knight of Grace of the Order of St John of Jerusalem.

Politically, Leslie was a staunch and active Unionist, although Warren (or 'Warnie') Lewis, brother of C S Lewis, recorded that "professional visits to our house [Little Lea on Circular Road] generally ended in he and my father passing a vote of no confidence in the Government of the day". Dr Leslie was Medical Adviser to the

Ulster Unionist Council during the years of the Home Rule Crisis before the First World War and he signed Sheet 41 of the Solemn League & Covenant (September 1912) at Belmont Presbyterian Church where he and his family worshipped.

Local Doctor

As the personal physician to many families in the East Belfast district, during the War he attended to a number of wounded soldiers to whom he demonstrated a sympathetic disposition. Lieut Arthur Temple Blackwood, an officer in the East Belfast Volunteers (8 Bn Royal Irish Rifles) – whose family lived at Saxonia on the Holywood Road, and who were very closely associated with the Ulster Bank at Mountpottinger – had suffered a shrapnel wound in the left shoulder on the first day of the Battle of the Somme. Two of Leslie's nephews who were pupils at Campbell College – Robert Cecil Wallace and James Lytton Millar – were killed within two months of one another during the War. The latter, at the age of 18, was the youngest Campbell pupil to be killed in action.

Medical bills outstanding upon his death reveal that Dr Leslie ministered to many of the well-known families in East Belfast. Mrs Margaret McNeill (who lived Lisnadene on Belmont Road), widow of the first Headmaster of Campbell College, owed the doctor £8 10s. Mrs MacDermott, widow of the former long-serving minister of Belmont Presbyterian Church, seems to have called upon his services more frequently, as her debt totalled £25. An inventory of the Leslie household drawn up at the time of his death shows that his most valuable possession was a 1927 Hillman Coupé – assessed at £30 – and Warren Lewis claimed that "Until quite late in life he was to be seen in all weathers making his extensive rounds on a bicycle".

Richard Whytock Leslie and solicitor Albert J Lewis reciprocated their professional skills but, whilst the sons of the latter (C S and

Warren) conceded that their family doctor was "a kindly and hard-working practitioner", they portrayed him as "an exquisitely ludicrous figure on a public occasion". Although he appears to have been a competent singer in public, his high, falsetto voice caused immense humour amongst the pupils of Campbell College, who christened him 'Squeaky Dick'. Warren Lewis stated that: "He was, I suspect, a good deal of a fool ... The neighbourhood grumbled at his inefficiency, [yet] sent for him regularly whenever it felt ill ... As a physician ... whether you were suffering from influenza, a broken arm, or a stomach ache, you might rest assured that the concluding instructions for your regimen would contain the words: 'and I should keep off eggs'". His reading matter, sneered Lewis, "degenerated from the novels of Guy Boothby to those of Zane Grey". Off-duty, the physician's pastimes were listed as horticulture (particularly botany), tennis, chess and bridge, to which, taunted the elder son of Little Lea, "it may be added that he at one period set up as an amateur of the Fine Arts, and a picture collector; but having been persuaded to purchase an oleograph as an original oil painting, he thereafter dropped the role of the virtuoso".

In June 1927 Albert Lewis fell prey to lumbago, which left him prostrate for over a fortnight. His younger son, by then established at Oxford, urged his father to avail himself of the expertise of his (Albert's) nephew, Joseph Tegart Lewis – of Sandycroft in the Bloomfield district – who had been a contemporary pupil with his cousin (C S Lewis) at Campbell, and later became a highly-regarded physician and bacteriologist in Belfast: "Certainly if the choice is between Squeaky and Joey, one can't hesitate. I hope you will commit yourself to the 'blood specialist's' hands from this day forth and profit by it".

Leslie became the longest-surviving member of the original staff of Campbell College. Following a scare over an outbreak of scarlatina in 1899 he recommended the complete sterilisation and disinfection of the school, and was consequently given 50 guineas "for his valuable services", and in late 1918 he ordered double inoculations during the influenza pandemic. He also ministered to two Headmasters who died in office (1907 and 1922). He was, however, prone to accept rather uncritically the efficacy of what he perceived to be a universal panacea. In the early twentieth century iodine was used as a remedy for many ailments, and it was asserted by William MacQuitty (the producer of the film *A Night to Remember*) that it was once employed at Belmont to paint a boy's feet – as a cure for his somnambulism!

Family Man

As a result of his marriage in 1889 to Rosa Scott Alexander of Londonderry, Richard Whytock Leslie had five daughters (all born in Belfast between 1892 and 1900). The names which they gave their third daughter is a hint that Rosa may have been related to William Alexander, Bishop of Derry (1867-1896) and later Archbishop of Armagh (1896-1911), and his wife, Cecil Frances, who composed such well-known hymns as *There is a Green Hill Far Away, All Things Bright and Beautiful* and the carol, *Once in Royal David's City*. Rosa Leslie was described by Warren Lewis as "a little, foolish, gushing woman, who had been pretty; she would have been a snob, had not her lack of sophistication blunted her snobbery into a laughable foible. When the last of her daughters had made a very ordinary local marriage, she announced in several Strandtown drawing rooms her satisfaction that 'All her girls were launched in Society'".

The most notable of these marriages was that of the second daughter, Gwendolen Agnes, on 5 March 1917 to Major Lennox George Brydges Rodney, who was a member of the family of Baron Rodney, and twenty years her senior. The marriage was inevitably conducted at Belmont Presbyterian Church by the minister and family friend, Rev Dr John MacDermott, with two of her sisters, Margaret Gladys and Frances – called 'Frank' in the *Belfast News Letter*! – as bridesmaids. The reception was held at the family home. By that time, the fourth daughter had died. Florence Elizabeth Henderson Leslie for some unspecified reason, committed suicide (by hanging) at St Heliers on 2 October 1914, aged seventeen. The house was subsequently rumoured to be haunted, an assertion repeated even by some of those who used the building towards the end of its life in the very early years of the twenty-first century, when it was owned by Short Bros & Harland Staff Supervisors' Club. Gladys (and probably her siblings) was well-known in East Belfast; C S Lewis records a note of irritation in his diary on 3 January 1923 that he was reduced to playing Cutthroat instead of Bridge because she had failed to turn up at Lisnadene, the McNeill home.

Dr Leslie composed his will on one rather scruffy, hand-written page on 6 July 1919, leaving everything to his wife, and asking that she subsequently divide it equally between his surviving daughters. He died on 22 September 1931, four days short of his sixty-ninth birthday. His outstanding debts included six guineas to the UVF Hospital at Craigavon House on Circular Road, and £20 to the Sans Souci Nursing Home on the Malone Road, where he probably died. Other debts included sums to Anderson McAuley department store, Sharman D Neill (jewellers in Royal Avenue) and William Mullan, the booksellers from whom he probably made his purchases as – in Warren Lewis's phrase – "an assiduous reader of trash". An extensive inventory of the contents of his house revealed little of individual material value – even eight Chippendale chairs were estimated at only £21 – but it did include, valued at three guineas, "a presentation clock from Campbell College" which he must have received only two months previously. According to one former pupil, he concealed "acute physical pain during the last few months of his life". There is a memorial plaque to Dr Richard Whytock Leslie in the Entrance Hall of Campbell College.

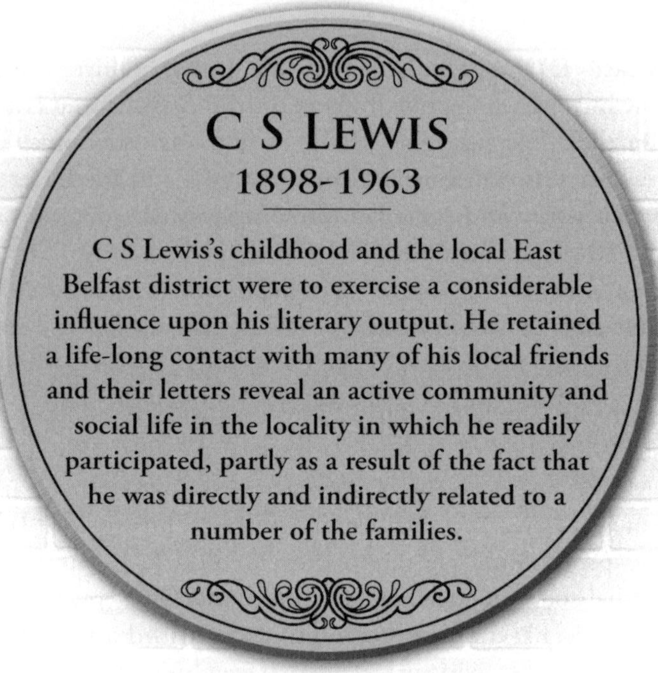

For all his international fame, his celebrated Oxbridge scholarship and his prodigious and diverse literary output, C S (or Jack, as he preferred) Lewis was ineradicably rooted in the life and society of East Belfast. Even when he was away from the family home at Little Lea on Circular Road – whether at school, at war, at university as an undergraduate or a don – he remained in regular correspondence with family, friends and acquaintances.

The impression the district made upon him proved indelible; one author has commented that "the turbulent democracy of little hills that is the County Down landscape exerted an irresistible heightening of awareness on Jack … The Irish landscape also provided a concrete link with his past and an endless source of imaginative inspiration". It is argued that the latter is evident in *The Magician's Nephew* (one of the *Chronicles of Narnia*): "All Narnia … lay spread out below them, the river winding through it like a ribbon of quicksilver (the Lagan). They could already see over the tops of the low hills which lay northward on their right (the Antrim hills) … On their left (southward) the mountains were much higher (the Mountains of Mourne), but every now and then there was a gap when you could see a glimpse of the southern lands that lay beyond (the Irish Republic)".

Secrets and Contradictions

Lewis could be extremely secretive, certainly private, about various aspects of his life, particularly about his probably adulterous relationship with the first woman with whom he lived for many years, Jane Moore, and even about his marriage to Joy Gresham. It is also evident that Lewis kept his two lives discrete; his world at Belmont and his professional life rarely, if ever, collided. Relatives, friends and casual social acquaintances from the former, however, feature constantly in his enduring correspondence with East Belfast.

His life also exhibited a number of contradictions. He had a few close friends at Belmont such as the corpulent Janie McNeill (daughter of a close family friend, James Adams McNeill, who had been the first Headmaster at Campbell College; see separate entry) and the homosexual Arthur Greeves (a neighbour of Little Lea who corresponded with Lewis for half a century). He visited the McNeill home on Belmont Road regularly when he was in Belfast, often playing bridge; he even dedicated his science novel *That Hideous Strength* to her in 1945.

When the Lewis family moved from Dundela to Circular Road in 1905, it was a nascent residential locality – you could still see Belfast Lough and the Antrim Hills from the house. The only neighbouring house was Bernagh, owned by Joseph Greeves, and when Jack's father installed a telephone in 1907 the first person his son rang was the youngest Greeves child, Arthur. Yet despite theirs remaining a life-time friendship, Lewis could not resist occasional caustic and sardonic comments at the expense of Arthur and his family.

There was one exception – again part of Lewis's secret world. When he started to gather their correspondence for editing in the early 1930s, Lewis promised his erstwhile neighbour that he would suppress all letters which related to 'It' – by which he meant Arthur's homosexuality. Lewis found no interest in this proclivity, but he suffered all the customary sexual angst which prevailed during teenage years – and his principal fixation was Arthur's sister, Lily. In February 1917, when Lewis was 18 years old and Lily was a few years older, he seems to have developed a mild sado-masochistic interest in punishment with the whip! He suggested to Arthur that Lily "could be punished in another way – to the general enjoyment of the operator and the great good of her soul … you must agree with me; is she not absolutely perfect from head to heel and moreover the necessary part of her body – one of the most beautiful parts anyway – shaped with an intolerable grace?" Four months later his suppressed obsession came embarrassingly to the fore. In his first term at Oxford he was invited to attend a dinner to celebrate the first class degree of E R Dodds (a former pupil at Campbell who had been expelled in 1912). Lewis confided to Arthur: "for the first time in my life, I was royally drunk. I am afraid that I must have given myself away rather as I went round imploring everyone to let me whip them for the sum of one shilling a lash"!

In 1918 Lily rescued herself by marrying Gordon Ewart (also a former pupil at Campbell) who lived at Schomberg on the Belmont Road. He was a son of Sir William Quartus Ewart (of nearby Glenmachan) who was, by marriage, a relation of C S Lewis. The Lewis brothers were invited round to the mansion regularly and in later life Jack conceded that "We had a standing invitation whenever we were at home; to this, almost entirely, we owe it that we did not grow up savages … Whatever I know (it is not much) of courtesy and *savoir faire* I learned [at Glenmachan]". Many years later Lewis informed Arthur that "I never pass a day without remembering you and the Glenmachonians and the McNeills", and following the Luftwaffe raids in May 1941 he bemoaned that "It's like the end of the world to think of bombs near Schomberg".

School Days

The social round was integral, almost *de rigueur*, to Belmont life, and Lewis was to boast that "we Strandtown and Belmont people had among us much kindness, wit, beauty and taste as any circle ... than I have ever known". His correspondence and memoirs reveal the games of literary charades, bridge and the banjo parties with Jimmy Thompson at Penrhyn (see entry for R L Thompson). It was this carousel which resulted in Jack's arrival at Campbell – if only for ten weeks – in September 1910.

Jack's mother had been very friendly with James Adams McNeill, the first Headmaster of Campbell College, who died suddenly in 1907. On 8 February 1910, Jack's father, Albert, met McNeill's successor, Robert MacFarland, at dinner at the rectory of St Mark's Church on the Holywood Road where the Lewis family were members of the congregation. They had been invited by Rev Gerald Peacocke, who had succeeded Rev Thomas Hamilton (Jack's maternal grandfather), who was sending his own son to the school.

As Lewis stayed for only ten weeks at Campbell before being removed to Malvern, commentators have been dismissive of his time at the school. The truth was, as his brother pointed out, that Jack did not find any of his educational establishments congenial and, whilst sociable, he was alienated from his fellow pupils. Nevertheless at least five of his cousins attended Campbell, one of whom – described by Jack as "my clever cousin" – was a contemporary on the Belmont estate His memories of Campbell, in fact, were not unfavourable, and it is significant that it is the only school whose name is not disguised in his autobiography, *Surprised by Joy*. He recalled his English teacher, Lewis Alden (see separate entry), with much affection and was always grateful to be introduced to Matthew Arnold's atmospheric poem, *Sohrab & Rustam*, which may well have helped to stimulate his later enthusiasm for medieval and esoteric literature.

Mysteries

The secretive, obscurantist approach of Lewis was applied equally to his literary output, and mysteries remain. Recent research by Michael Ward in *Planet Narnia* has revealed that the somewhat random and disjointed composition of the seven tales of Narnia, ostensibly written for children, has a much more subtle and philosophical relationship based upon medieval cosmology – which was never revealed by Lewis.

It has been demonstrated that, in addition to the topographical impact the locality had upon his work, other 'landmarks' filtered into his sub-consciousness – such as the door handle featuring the lion's head on the old rectory of St Mark's, which is claimed to be the inspiration for Aslan. It is also asserted that Campbell College provided the sentinel to Narnia, which "lies between the lamp-post and the great castle of Cair Paravel on the Eastern Sea" – a gas lamp-post which still adorns the main driveway into Campbell. Although there is a plausibility in the idea that this was Lewis's inspiration, sadly there is no evidence for it. It is an old lamp-post which lit the way to Belmont House, which Campbell replaced in 1894. It was manufactured in Scotland and probably installed by Belmont's erstwhile occupant, Sir Thomas McClure (see separate entry), and disconnected with the abandonment of the house. The estate and the streets of Belmont were replete with standard gas-lamps and it is possible that the one which had most influence upon C S Lewis was the one outside Little Lea, which he specifically refers to beaming into his room on his last night in the house before he sold it to Samuel Johnston (see entry for Elliott Johnston).

There is one mystery, nevertheless, to which no-one seems to be able to offer an explanation. In 1932 the Lewis brothers presented a stained-glass window to St Mark's Church in memory of their parents. The main content, three saints, has a relevance, but along the bottom are displayed fractured aspects of houses and buildings, the significance of which nobody has yet explained. Perhaps one day, as with Michael Ward's epiphany with regard to *The Chronicles of Narnia*, this secret will be revealed.

F A Lewis

1862-1908

Born in Cork (as was her husband, Albert), Flora Lewis was the mother of C S Lewis. Both her commitment to her sons' education, and her early death, were to have an influence upon the author's childhood, his relationship with his father and his literary output. She died from cancer at the age of forty-six.

Florence Hamilton (usually known as Flora) was born in Cork in May 1862. Her father, Rev Thomas Hamilton, had attempted the Grand Tour of Europe in 1850 and between 1852 and 1853 travelled to Calcutta in the hope of improving his health. For four years from 1870 he took his family of two sons and two daughters to Rome where he was chaplain at Holy Trinity Church. In 1874 he was appointed Rector at the recently founded St Mark's Church (consecrated in 1878) on the Holywood Road at Sydenham until his retirement in 1900.

Although by that stage older than most school pupils, Flora attended classes at Methodist College between 1881 and 1885, where she was taught by James Adams McNeill, the future Headmaster of Campbell College, and the most outstanding Mathematics teacher on the island, and McNeill was later to claim that Flora was "the cleverest girl pupil he ever had". She became the first female Mathematics graduate (with an excellent degree) at Queen's College in Belfast (erroneously called Queen's University in *The Dictionary of Irish Biography*).

She was acquainted with her future husband from her earliest days at Sydenham and Strandtown, as Albert Lewis (who coincidentally was also born in Cork) was a parishioner at St Mark's. She rejected a proposal of marriage from his brother, William, in 1886, which appears to have emboldened Albert's own approaches to her; it was, however, seven years before she agreed to marry him, and they married at her father's church on 29 August 1894. The first part of their honeymoon was spent at Betws-y-Coed in Wales.

They originally lived at Dundela Villas on Dundela Avenue before moving in 1905 to Little Lea, a house commissioned by Albert on Circular Road in Belmont. Flora was generous enough to accommodate her father-in-law at both homes between 1903 and 1908. The younger son, C S (Jack) Lewis (see separate entry), always felt that the new home was a badly-designed and draughty and, after his father's death in 1928, regarded it as almost unsaleable. The family was nevertheless socially grounded in the district, as Lady Ewart at Glenmachan was Flora's first cousin. Flora's sister, Lily Suffern, was an ardent suffragette and an ally to the wife of the artist, Alfred Rawlings Baker, who lived at Knock junction, and whom C S Lewis was to characterise as "a violent suffragette".

Although Lily argued with all members of the family, Flora appears to have proved more sociable and sedate. Her sons recalled knitting as one of her pastimes and, more surprisingly, stamp collecting, although when her sons sold her collection in 1929 some of the 'best' stamps were found to be forgeries and it raised only £4. Flora took a close interest in the education of Jack and Warren and, in their younger years, taught them French and Latin. Even at a young age, Jack was to demonstrate an advanced vocabulary and literary tastes. She endeavoured to foster broader horizons, and took them on holiday (Albert hated vacations), as in 1901 to Castlerock and (for the final time) in 1907 to Berneval near Dieppe.

She was diagnosed with cancer in February 1908 and died on her husband's birthday, 23 August 1908. She was buried in the City Cemetery. Her younger son kept her private desk at his Oxford home, the Kilns, but he seems to have been disinclined to give the woman with whom he lived, Jane Moore, any of his mother's jewellery. Although 1929 was not a propitious time to sell such articles, the sum raised was donated to the commission and installation of the window to both parents in St Mark's in 1935.

The sudden death of Flora Lewis had a profound impact on Albert and his two sons and greatly affected their relationship. It is arguable that, if C S Lewis had enjoyed a much longer period with his mother, he may not have had to entertain and occupy himself to such a great extent, and his literary output and creativity may well have proved notably different.

Percy McElwaine's grandfather was a native of Larne who later settled in Coleraine, where his son, Adam John, was born. The latter flourished as a typical Presbyterian who embraced Liberal Unionism and hailed, as his son (Percy) was to affirm, from "that solid reliable stock which has produced the North of Ireland man, a stock remarkable for its puritanism, self-reliance, independence and perseverance". Percy's imperial pride was also evident later in life when he attended the coronation ceremony in May 1937. The Ulster character was also manifested in the response to Percy's second marriage: "Mother, and I think Father, took a liking to Madge at once, but Father could not get over my marrying a Roman Catholic [albeit from the West Indies] and it grieved Mother greatly too". Nevertheless, in the post-Partition period Adam McElwaine and his wife were perfectly happy to reside in Dundalk and Dublin.

Education

Shortly after 1875 McElwaine senior became a Schools Inspector which necessitated relocation to various parts of Ireland and Percy was born on 21 September 1884 in Roscommon. At the end of February 1900 Adam McElwaine's duties took him to Knock and the family became the first occupants of a newly-built semi-detached property on Hawthornden Road which they named Dalkeith. Percy confessed that he was, for many years, an educational disappointment to his father but his later work-rate became prodigious, and he recorded that when studying for his Moderatorship (final examinations) at TCD in 1907 he "studied ten or twelve hours per day". He was called to the Irish Bar on 9 June 1908.

He read extensively and reflectively, as was made evident by the many submissions which he offered to a noted literary journal. In 1912 his observations on a man convicted in Clonmel in 1895 for the burning of his wife as a witch indicated that the young barrister recognised early in his career the problems of the co-existence of common law (including custom and superstition) and statute law. This uncomfortable fusion was readily apparent in a number of the courts he experienced in various parts of the Commonwealth; in Kenya, for instance, he found that instances of death and murder were complicated by the belief in magic and bewitchment.

First World War

Whilst in retrospect the success of Percy McElwaine's legal career appears to have been mapped out by destiny, revealing a continuous progression, culminating in his knighthood consequent upon his office as Chief Justice of the Straits Settlement (Singapore, 1936-1946), initially he had struggled to gain entry to the Colonial Civil Service. In order to obtain some of the requisite experience, he departed in April 1913 for Canada, establishing his own legal firm in Edmonton, a town which he discovered boasted a substantial Irish population. He quickly absorbed the idiosyncrasies of the Canadian legal system and was called to the Alberta Bar in October 1913.

By July 1915 the lawyer decided to enlist in the British Armed Forces via the Inns of Court OTC. He was gazetted a probationary 2nd Lieut in the Royal Irish Rifles on 5 August 1916, becoming a temporary Lieut on 5 February 1918. He served on the Western Front from October 1916 with 'B' Coy of 14 Battalion Royal Irish Rifles (Young Citizen Volunteers), which was commanded at that time by well-known Belmont character and former fellow pupil, Major James McKee DSO (see separate entry). On 17 June 1916 he married Evelyn McNaught of whom he had been considerably enamoured for three or four years. Over the next two years he saw little of his wife and, to his great distress, on the day before the War officially ended, without him being able to return home in time, she became a victim of the 1918 influenza pandemic.

McElwaine rarely experienced front line action. He admitted that "I was too theoretical to make a good regimental officer". This analytical mind was, however, put to a creative legal use which antagonised his superiors, who retaliated by appointing to him what they regarded as tedious bureaucractic and administrative posts. Shortly after his Commission in 1916 he was posted to the newly-formed 19 (Reserve Battalion) Royal Irish Rifles based at Newcastle. Whilst there, as Company orderly, he was asked to hear the case of a soldier disobeying an order; his legal training caused the case to be dropped, as no witnesses were produced. He also obtained a number of acquittals in Courts-Martial on the grounds of lack of substantive evidence or on a technicality. McElwaine reasoned that soldiers appreciated a fair trial "and that more often than not discipline is improved rather than weakened by the acquittal". Such success rates resulted in the Divisional HQ appointing him to a distant posting in Amiens as Divisional Purchasing

Officer which, as he admitted, meant that he had "a nice comfortable billet ... while the Division was engaged in the snows and Battle of Cambrai".

His innate sense of justice and fairness were evident in his observation of one death in the Ypres/Messines sector where he was based: "Willie Redmond MP, who was serving as an officer in the 16 (Irish) Division, was wounded and was brought into one of the Field Ambulances where he died [7 June 1917]. He was far too old for soldiering [at 56] but we all respected him, political enemy though he was. I attended his funeral at Locre Convent".

Island Service

After the War his legal business in Edmonton had failed but, after further application to the Colonial Service, he was approached in May 1920 and asked if he would consider the post of Magistrate Recorder in St Lucia in the West Indies. Despite the disapproval of his father who felt that it was not sufficiently paid, the ambitious lawyer seized the opportunity to place his foot on the bottom rung of the Colonial ladder. Thereafter, until after the Second World War, his career was spent on various imperial (or Commonwealth) islands around the globe.

He was to serve for two years on the Windward Island where he struggled to streamline and accelerate its judicial system. On 23 January 1923 he married Margaret (Madge) Belmar, the daughter of a former planter, before arriving three months later in Kenya where he had been appointed Senior Crown Counsel. As Senior Crown Counsel "I did most of the criminal work and a considerable amount of advising and drafting of regulations and some bills"; amongst the latter was a short Bill for the protection of coconuts! He felt that the judicial process was hampered by a belief in superstition and magic, and his memoirs are a fertile record of such peculiarities under imperial authority. In late 1927 he accepted the position of Attorney General in Fiji where, via a stop in Australia, he settled in January 1928. He worked on the island for just over two years – drafting legislation, advising the Government and presenting Assizes, in addition to helping to revise the Constitution which dated back to the 1860s.

Singapore

In mid-1930 McElwaine accepted the post of Deputy Public Prosecutor in Singapore and by late 1933 had been appointed Attorney General. In August 1936 he published his five volume *Revised Edition of the Ordinances of the Straits Settlement.*

In February 1936 he took a fortnight's leave to visit Hong Kong, which proved to be a 'small world' experience. The journey back to Singapore was on board *SS Rawalpindi*, a P&O vessel built at Harland & Wolff. The captain, Ralph Beck, had been a fellow pupil at Campbell College who lived on North Road at Bloomfield. McElwaine was also acquainted with three other men at the Chief Officer's table, including an (unnamed) officer who lived at Knock. The *Rawalpindi* had a fatal attraction for erstwhile pupils from Belmont: Thomas Fee of Holywood served an apprenticeship at Harland & Wolff in the years after leaving Campbell in 1921, and in late 1939 was on board the requisitioned liner as a Lieut in the Royal Naval Reserve when it was sunk off the coast of Iceland by two German battleships. Ironically, Fee managed to escape on a lifeboat, but it was overloaded and all on board drowned when it was capsized by a wave.

Later in 1936 he became Chief Justice of the Straits Settlement, a post traditionally accompanied by a knighthood, which he received in January 1939. In August 1939 he took delivery of a new Supreme Court, but had little time to enjoy or appreciate it before the Japanese invasion of Singapore and its surrender on 15 February 1942, which its leading judicial figure described as "the blackest and most disgraceful day in our history". Although he had ensured the departure of his family, he was imprisoned – along with 2700 others in space for 700 men, on a 90% rice diet – in Changi gaol. The invasion also cost him his private prized library. McElwaine was later moved to other internment camps where three years of enforced leisure provided him with the opportunity to devour reams of literature, including the complete works of Shakespeare. Eventually liberated from Manchuria in August 1945, he observed that "For years my job was to supply tenants for Singapore [Changi] gaol. I never expected to be one myself".

In 1948, as Commissioner, Sir Percy produced a *Report on the Administration of the Income Tax Department* in Sierra Leone, and followed this six years later by editing the *Revised Edition of the Laws of the Gold Coast*. Sir Percy retired to Teignmouth in Devon and died there on 24 October 1969.

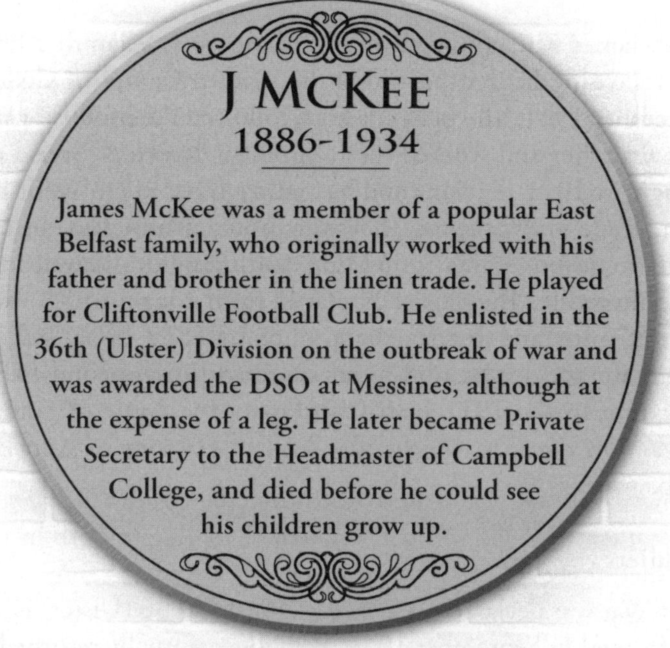

Life was particularly unkind on a number of occasions to James McKee (as it was to his older brother, William Dickson McKee) but, as one who knew him well recorded at his death, "he never complained". The brothers were the sons of Samuel McKee who originally lived on Earlswood Road, but later moved to 35 Cyprus Park, and made his living, as did so many in East Belfast, from the linen trade. The family were well-known at their place of worship, Belmont Presbyterian Church, where even as teenagers the boys helped to run the Boys' Brigade unit. Not all of the family members were enthralled by the lengthy sermons of Rev Dr John MacDermott (minister from 1880 until 1920), and – until it was removed during later renovations – the family pew long bore the teeth imprint of a bored sister!

Both boys attended Belmont National School, originally attached to the church, which in August 1890 was relocated to new premises and renamed Ferguson Memorial School on the Belmont

Road. James was a pupil there from January 1895 until 1899, before following his brother along the road to Campbell College in September 1901. The brothers both followed the professional path of their father and worked for John Shaw Brown & Sons Ltd, although in 1911 William and his father travelled to work briefly in the trade in Argentina. They were both enthusiastic sportsmen: William played cricket for YMCA and they both played football for Cliftonville. The older boy played for the team which won the Steel & Sons and Intermediate Cups in 1899-1900, but James played for the senior team, and came within a second replay of appearing in the 1911 Irish Cup Final. The name of James also appears on the First World War Roll of Honour of Knock Golf Club.

Soldiers

After War was declared on 4 August 1914 and 36 (Ulster) Division was formed in September 1914, William eventually returned from Argentina to enlist and received a commission in 12 Royal Irish Rifles on 15 March 1915. He was mentioned in despatches in *The London Gazette* (12 August 1916) for his role in the attack on Liberty Hall in Dublin during the Easter Rising 1916. He participated in the Battle of the Somme (July 1916) and at Messines Ridge (June 1917), but was killed on 12 August 1917 during the mud-ridden Battle of Passchendaele. His name appears on Panel 40 of the Menin Gate, but he is believed to have been buried near the Pommern Redoubt.

James spent two years in the Young Citizen Volunteers, established by Campbell's neighbour at Cabin Hill, the Lord Mayor of Belfast, Robert McMordie, and run by Campbell Governor and gun-runner, Fred Crawford. When war was declared it transformed into 14 Royal Irish Rifles in which James rose to become a captain. He was a considerate officer, recorded in the regimental magazine, *The Incinerator*, as one of those who made at Christmas 1915 "a pilgrimage round the billets to … see how the men were enjoying the geese, duck, fowl and last, but not least, the Christmas plum pudding".

He was present at the opening day of the Somme when William McFadzean sacrificed his own life to save his comrades from fallen grenades. As the private's company officer, McKee took responsibility for notifying the father who lived at Rubicon (now a doctor's surgery) at the top of the Cregagh Road in East Belfast, and was one of those instrumental in obtaining the Victoria Cross for the fallen soldier. He related the circumstances to Mr McFadzean, saying that "You will have the satisfaction of knowing that [your son] died a hero's death … He saved the lives of a number of comrades by his action ... His name has been sent forward to higher authority with recommendation for a decoration".

He was present at Messines Ridge with his brother, but never made it Passchendaele, as he lost a leg on the ridge on 7 June 1917 and was shipped home a week later. He was moved to hospital in Liverpool and then to the Dublin Castle Hospital. *The London Gazette* (17 September 1917) recorded the award to him of the DSO "for conspicuous gallantry and devotion to duty in leading his company in an attack. Although wounded he continued to advance until severely wounded for a second time, his leg being so badly shattered that it has since been amputated. He has at all times led his men with compete disregard of personal danger, and the splendid training which he had instilled into them beforehand proved its worth in enabling them to gain and hold their objective under trying circumstances". He received the medal at Buckingham Palace on 11 May 1918. In March 1918 he was also awarded the Croix de Guerre, confirmed upon him by the King of the Belgians.

On 10 August 1917 he was granted a wound pension of £100 per annum, which he felt did not reflect the seriousness of the wound and the permanent incapacity which he had suffered. He wrote to the War Office on 12 November from the UVF Hospital at Gilford (Co Down) to say that, in addition to the amputation, he had fractured both bones in his left arm which was now shorter and did not have full movement – requesting an additional £100. Hearing nothing, he wrote again twice in June 1918, but there is no indication that he ever received the additional sum. He was obliged to relinquish his commission on the grounds of ill-health caused by wounds, but was granted the right to retain the honorary rank of Captain. At the time of McKee's death in 1934, the Headmaster of Campbell College, Duff Gibbon, who had also won the DSO in the First World War, praised his resilience: "Sometimes he suffered pain and discomfort from his old wound, but he never complained and never let other people's comfort be upset by his discomfort".

Civilian Life

In 1925 he became Private Secretary to Gibbon at Campbell College, where he remained a very popular figure. In his tribute, the Headmaster said that McKee's attitude to life was "sympathy with everybody, quiet humour at all times, modesty with regard to his own achievements, courtesy to all". He married Dorothy Colton in 1925 and (apart from a daughter who died after a few weeks) had two sons, James (always known as Jasper from an early age) and Ian. Unfortunately he never lived to see them go to school, as fate struck him another blow when he died on 14 July 1934 at the Botanic House Private Nursing Home from complications following an operation for appendicitis and gallstones.

After a short service at the school, the Campbell College Pipe Band lined the street outside his home at 33 Stormont Park to play the Last Post and Reveille before his burial at Dundonald Cemetery. Both his sons were educated in East Belfast; the younger worked for the United Nations, and Jasper, the elder son, is a renowned physicist and former Director of the Cyclotron Laboratory at the University of Manitoba in Winnipeg.

E L MacNaghten

1879-1942

Edmund MacNaghten was educated in East Belfast and adopted a career in the Church. He was invalided out of the Army in the First World War, and stood as a failed Independent Nationalist in Londonderry. He practised osteopathy before returning to an ecclesiastical career, but was to fall out with his Bishop.

Some families seem destined to attract adversity and misfortune and one of these was the MacNaghten clan of Bushmills, whose family motto – *I hope in God* – often proved mistakenly optimistic.

Edmund Loftus MacNaghten (born 14 December 1879) and his brother, Steuart Cecil MacNaghten (born 4 October 1881), lived at Sandown Villa on the Sandown Road in Knock during the final years of the 19th century. Their great-grandfather, Sir Francis Workman MacNaghten of Bushmills, had been a judge in Madras and Calcutta, and their grandfather, Francis MacNaghten, had worked in the Bengal Civil Service. The latter's four sons at one stage all earned their living on the Indian sub-continent. The father of Edmund and Steuart, Steuart Lambert MacNaghten, had married Caroline Matilda Garstin in Muzaffarpur in Bihar province on 11 December 1878. The two boys were probably born in Bombay (now Mumbai).

Edmund and his brother were educated at Campbell College during its second academic year (1895-1896); during that period Edmund became a member of the school's very first cricket XI (for which the future detective writer, Freeman Wills Crofts, was the scorer) and on 30 May 1896 made the first half-century scored by a Campbellian. It is not clear where he continued his education after 1896, but he appears to have attended TCD, and to have qualified in 1902 as a clergyman at Ely Theological College. During the next nine years he held a number of ecclesiastical posts as at Norwich and Chelsea. This included a single year (1904-1905) as the first resident rector at St Monica's Church in Lamerton, Alberta. It was then effectively a shack on the Canadian prairies although, as one of the three oldest churches in Alberta, it is now designated a historic site.

Military Service

Some sources indicate that Edmund then adopted a career as an osteopath, but he was never registered with the professional body, and must have practised in an amateur, unofficial capacity. On 2 June 1915, whilst resident in Deal (Kent), he applied for a Commission in the Regular Army, nominating the Army Service Corps Mechanical Transport. He obtained the Commission as 2nd Lieut five days later, and after two months was promoted to Lieut. He served in an active capacity for only six months before being invalided out of service between 27 January and 29 July 1916. Following a bout of dysentery, he appears to have contracted colitis and dyspepsia, which he later claimed "changed me from an absolutely sound and healthy man into a crock, who is nearly always in pain and never free from grave discomfort". MacNaghten effectively remained an invalid for the rest of the War. He was appointed a temporary Captain on 13 December 1917 in the Corps of Royal Engineers, but resigned his Commission (retaining the honorary rank of Captain) on 25 September 1918 "on account of ill-health".

Irish Politics

Edmund MacNaghten next surfaces in the pages of history controversially on the political scene. Despite being, as he claimed, "an Ulsterman and a Protestant", by 1922 he had adopted an anti-Unionist philosophy. Described by *The Northern Whig* as "a strange Ulsterman", Edmund campaigned for the Londonderry constituency at the 1922 General Election. Bizarrely, most of his canvassing appears to have been undertaken in the United States, in locations as far apart as San Francisco and Boston. In the latter he declared that: "Right at the very door of England, in her home, she is crushing Ireland through the very system she fought [in the Great War] to crush in others ... Ireland, our Ireland, is in fetters and chains. Crimes unheard-of in history are witnessed daily in Ireland today".

Sinn Fein doubted his nationalist credentials and disowned him, so he stood as an Independent Nationalist against the Unionist candidate, Sir Malcolm MacNaghten – who was his cousin! The Unionist heavyweights, including Captain Charles Craig MP, chairman of the Ulster Parliamentary party at Westminster, who had lived at the family home, Craigavon on Circular Road, all backed Sir Malcolm. Edmund conducted one meeting at St Columb's Hall in Derry on the Sunday before the General Election, which was held on 16 November 1922. Surprisingly, he polled a respectable near-10,000 votes in the gerrymandered constituency and arrived in Derry to concede the seat, when he wished his cousin's politics "speedy and complete defeat"!

Final Years

The next years were spent in obscurity, perhaps practising osteopathy to earn a living, but in 1938 he accepted the incumbency of Stanhoe with Barwick, a small village in the diocese of Norwich. Maintaining his practice of not gracing any ecclesiastical appointment for more than a year or two, in 1939 Edmund became Vicar at St Thomas's Church at Overmonnow in Monmouth, as a consequence of his long-term acquaintance with Alfred Edwin Monahan, with whom he had been acquainted at TCD and who became Bishop of Monmouth in 1940. The vicar alienated his congregation as a result of his extreme Anglo-Catholicism and then antagonised his friend by refusing access to his church to the archdeacon who was sent to investigate. MacNaghten was charged with "insubordination to the archdeacon and a lack of discipline" and found guilty of unacceptable conduct. Whilst the judgement specified that his offence was not "a grave one", Monahan took exception and deprived him of his living. MacNaghten filed an appeal in September 1942, alleging "malice, personal ill will and animosity" on the part of the bishop, but he died towards the end of that year in the midst of the controversy, leaving his wife (Ethel Mary Scaife, whom he had married in 1912) to continue his cause. The ecclesiastical court showed little sympathy and eventually found against him.

Jane (or Janie, as she was customarily known) McNeill was the only child of James Adams McNeill and Margaret (née Cunningham, a member of the wealthy commercial Belfast family). When her father, who had previously been vice-principal at Methodist College, became Headmaster at Campbell College in 1894 the family lived on the school premises, and she was educated privately by two of the most able schoolmasters at Belmont, Roby Davis and Lewis Alden (see separate entry), before she attended Victoria College at the age of thirteen. These two instilled in her "a love of literature which never left her", and her friend C S Lewis (see separate entry) revealed her individual way of obtaining reading matter: using the book shop as a free library! She became extremely knowledgeable about Scottish ballads and poetry – particularly that of William Dunbar (died c.1513) – and it was claimed that she developed a profound acquaintance with medieval French literature.

In her youth she developed a close friendship with C S Lewis and Arthur Greeves, both of whom attended Campbell and lived in the first homes built on Circular Road. This relationship proved enduring, although the author of the tales of Narnia held a very ambivalent attitude towards her. In later years, in one of his innumerable letters to Arthur, he labelled Janie (or 'Tchanie' as he often referred to her, mimicking her mother's accent) "an appalling woman … profaning our sacred haunts [the Holywood Hills] and soaking our machines [bikes] with her constant chatter".

As Jane's father had been particularly well-disposed towards Lewis's mother, Lewis retained a close acquaintance with Jane and her mother, who lived at Lisnadene, 191 Belmont Road, after the Headmaster's sudden death in 1907. Lewis visited their home whenever he returned from Oxford, although he was to find their provincialism rather tedious. He suspected that Janie related apocryphal and invented tales, and once noted in his diary that he was invited to lunch: "I did not want to go, but I had no excuse ready and so accepted". The McNeill pair occasionally made visits to Oxford and in 1922 he recorded that he took Janie to tea but "I found her desperately boring – tho' in Ireland I have often regarded her as a bit of the larger world. She went over ancient stories, and explained [my brother's] psychology with a lavish display of ignorance. She is stagnating like the rest and falling back on matter which has been used over and over again … I am really sorry for her".

This observation was made in 1922 and, for all his reservations, it reflected a growing sympathy which he felt for her. Her education and intellect provided her with vision and aspiration. She spoke with Lewis "about her longing to get away from Strandtown" and, because of the necessity to provide company for her mother (who did not die until Christmas Day 1946), "the impossibility of doing so". He realised that "mentally she can just see beyond

Strandtown", adding that "of course there must be sexual despair as well". In later years he confided in Greeves that he had enjoyed one of her visits and "If there were any changes in her, I thought they were all for the better". At her passing on 24 March 1959, he went further: "We now miss her dreadfully; while she was alive what a lot of time we spent evading her"! In 1945 he dedicated his science-fiction work, That Hideous Strength, to her, but she loathed the book and said "I wish he had dedicated any book other than this to me".

Helen Waddell

Jane did occasionally venture beyond the United Kingdom. In 1924 she and her mother accompanied the future author of medieval themes such as *The Wandering Scholars and Peter Abelard*, Helen Waddell (who was the same age as Jane), on a motoring tour of Touraine in France. This adventure revealed the contradictory nature which the McNeills could present. One of the tributes to Jane was to claim that she had "a profound knowledge of the Bible" – but it was circumscribed by the parameters of ardent Presbyterianism, which were sustained to her final days in her last will and testament. The creator of Narnia also referred to her, unambiguously, as "a true, sometimes grim, daughter of the Kirk". When John Cook arrived at Belmont as the new Headmaster in 1954 she was a spectre at the gate, who continued to haunt the estate in an endeavour to ensure that he would maintain the Presbyterian character of her father's incumbency.

In her will she left the substantial sum of £14,000 to the Governors of Campbell College to fund two eponymous scholarships (set at £150) "to such of their pupils as may desire to proceed to a University and are likely to profit thereby and are in need of financial assistance". In later years this generosity created angst at the College, as she added the restrictive rider: "in view of the fact that Campbell College was built and endowed by a Presbyterian [Henry James Campbell], I direct that the Scholarships be awarded only to communicants of the Presbyterian Church in Ireland". It was not until 2012 that this clause was successfully legally altered, with the judge commenting that it was unlikely that anyone would change faith to meet the criteria, but "People have done it for anything from a bowl of soup to the crown of France"!

Jane's friendship with Helen Waddell probably stemmed from the fact that the latter's family was also Presbyterian. The future author had been born in Tokyo whilst her father carried out missionary work for the Presbyterian Church in Church (of which the Missions' Secretary was, coincidentally, the brother of McNeill's successor at Campbell, Robert MacFarland). Two of her brothers attended Campbell College in 1900. Evidently the relationship was a close one; when *The Wandering Scholars* was published in 1927, C S Lewis wrote to Arthur Greeves, asking: "Have you seen Helen Waddell's book? I am sure Tchanie is never tired of talking of it. It is specially interesting to us because, when you have read it, you see what an enormous influence H[elen] W[addell] had on Tchanie: the book is full of passages that Tchanie would have written herself if she could".

When the female party visited the medieval cathedral of Tours, somewhat out of character, they "went to High Mass … and Mrs McNeill knelt and bowed to the altar like a good Papist … When I talk to her about the Middle Ages, she listens as if I were the Ancient Mariner", reported Helen – who was to be rewarded by a £50 annuity in Mrs McNeill's will. Helen found herself amused by her companion's idiosyncrasies: "It's gone cold all at once, and Jane is triumphant because, in heat so fierce that I was sleeping with only a sheet, she packed woollen knickers and a burberry … Jane is really behaving awfully well. I hear a good deal of her own excellence as a traveller, till in self-defence I produced a rhyme which gets added to every day":

Jane or the Perfect Traveller
She likes to travel in the train,
She never smells an open drain.
On boats she talks to stewardesses,
And gives advice in their distresses.
She is not sick in any swell,
But only in each new hotel.
And even in Paris summer heat
she wears galoshes on her feet.

There must be the suspicion that Jane provided the template for Alberta Scrubb – the non-conformist, teetotal, non-smoking woman who wore "a special kind of underwear" – in the Narnian tale, The Voyage of the Dawn Treader.

A Lawnmower

By her middle years she had grown extremely corpulent, a condition compounded by being crippled and a reliance upon two sticks. She had visited C S Lewis's father, Albert, every day at Little Lea during his final illness (when she was only 40). With an acknowledgement of her physical plight, the Oxford don informed his brother: "You know the difficulty she finds in getting out of a room and, when that is conquered, the further difficulty of getting off a doorstep". In his final tribute to her, Lewis penned sympathetically: "When I consider how all this was maintained through years of increasing loneliness, pain, disability and inevitable frustration, I am inclined to say she had a soul as brave and uncomplaining as any I know".

Her attachment to the institution which her father had done most to mould remained – at times, irritatingly – staunch. She endeavoured, unsuccessfully, to have a house built in the grounds, and rattled round the 100-acre estate in an old car, accompanied by a noisy dog named Laddie, occasionally reporting errant pupils to the Headmaster. Nearly every beneficiary in her will was associated with Campbell College. In Northern Ireland her personal estate was valued at £9500, bolstered by real estate of £5400; she also held a personal estate of £22,000 in England and Wales.

Her place of worship, Belmont Presbyterian Church, was graced with a £300 donation as an investment for the Minister's stipend fund. One of her executors was Frederick Douglas Bartley, a retired and decorated Calcutta police chief, whom she had probably befriended during her early education at Campbell; he also received £500. Her many books were bequeathed to a number of individuals, but priority choice was given to C S Lewis and his brother, Warren. She left a Crown Derby tea service to the wife of Ken Armour, a long-term member of staff at Campbell College who persuaded Lewis to produce the tribute for the school magazine. One of Armour's colleagues and wife – 'Taffy' and Rosalinde Ragg – were left £100 each, plus her lawnmower. It is uncertain what offence the latter pair may have caused her, but a codicil of December 1956 reversed the £100 bequests – although they seem to have retained the lawnmower!

The final comment on her from her celebrated friend claimed that "Few have come nearer to obeying [the Scottish poet] Dunbar's magnificent recipe":

Man, please thy Maker and be merry
And give not for this world a cherry.

Martha was one of only three of the eleven children of Rev Thomas Drennan, minister at Rosemary Street Presbyterian Church in Belfast, to survive to adulthood; the other two siblings were Nancy (1745-1825) and her more celebrated brother, William (1754-1820), one of the founders of the United Irishmen.

In 1773 she married Samuel McTier, a widowed Belfast chandler, who had one daughter (Margaret). It proved to be a happy, although childless, marriage, which one commentator described as "emotionally, intellectually and physically satisfying". Sam was not a great businessman but he appears to have been trustworthy, reliable and sociable – although it seems that he "enjoyed a good election riot". Their fortunes stabilised in 1785 when Sam was appointed as Ballast Master to the Harbour Commissioners and, with a loan of £50 from her brother, they purchased 31 acres at Knock and built a country retreat. Although they initially contemplated a number of bizarre names such as Mount Modicum, Badinage, Competence and even Try-it, they eventually named it Cabin Hill. (The original cottage was rebuilt in the 1860s by the Dinnen family and survives today).

Although, Martha became exceptionally fond of Cabin Hill, her early association with the cottage was short-lived. The focus of her husband's work was in Belfast, so much of their time was spent in their house in what is currently Donegall Square North (officially 4 South Parade), where Sam, William (her brother), Wolfe Tone and Thomas Russell will have spent some time discussing the formation and activities of the United Irishmen from late 1791. Her social circle was such that during the political upheaval in the late 1790s she dined with General Lake, the Commander-in-Chief in Ireland who had been sent to suppress the United Irishmen, and occasionally watched troops parading past her window.

Her first neighbours at Cabin Hill were the family of Richard Brown Bamber who lived at the adjacent estate of Belmont, with whom she seems to have enjoyed a sociable relationship; when William Drennan was acquitted of the charge of sedition in Dublin in 1794, it was one of Bamber's sons who first offered his congratulations at the Belfast home. Belmont, however, was purchased in 1788 by William Bateson (whose family were linked to neighbouring Orangefield) and who exhibited few social graces; Martha complained that the Batesons were a noisy and anti-social family and revealed that "If my father's cat were alive, I would rather have it for a neighbour"!

Unhappy Years and Recovery

Her middle years were marked by misfortune and unhappiness. She and Sam left Cabin Hill after only four years in 1789, when she appears to have suffered a nervous breakdown. At this stage her voluminous correspondence with her brother, which endured from

1776 until 1819, suffered a hiatus of three years. This coincided with the move from Newry to Dublin of William's medical practice which never proved financially successful, and she was troubled by the serious charges against him in 1794. Her husband died suddenly at Inveraray in May 1795 during their visit to Scotland. Sam had failed to make a will and this only accentuated her sense of insecurity and financial worries and for a brief period she lived with Sam's daughter, Margaret.

Martha, however, made a determined effort to restore her fortunes and to live independently. She visited her brother and his wife, Sarah, in Dublin, and was engaged in charitable work for poor women and children. She consciously involved herself in the social round, attending the theatre, balls and parties but, as one commentator notes, "although Martha had a wide circle of acquaintances, she disliked many of them and she had few close friends". Her spirit of independence was manifested in her enthusiasm for playing cards, which involved modest gambling, for which she was chided by her brother. In 1800 she indicated to William's wife that she had played whist, but suffered "a particular set of silly scolding virulent chiming old women" and changed to another game, casino; she claimed: "It interests me. I am politely treated, play as well as any of [the men], and when I lose too much I will quit it".

Despite such pastimes, she possessed an active intellect and read widely and seriously. The age was characterised by revolution, as in America and France, which was to have an impact upon political developments in Ireland which played a central part in the lives of her family and acquaintances, and she was familiar with the leading political philosophy of the age and debated it in depth in her correspondence, which brought her a reputation in some official quarters as "a republican". She also devoured religious history, biography, novels, poetry, radical newspapers and pamphlets.

Return to Cabin Hill

Her reading was, however, discriminating. Despite the fact that she knew Wolfe Tone, she was not enamoured of his 1790 mock-Gothic, satirical novel, Belmont Castle – the title of which can, nevertheless, only have accentuated her fond memories of the Knock locality – which lampooned figures from the Anglo-Irish establishment. She and her brother were also interested in the contemporary educational works of Maria Edgeworth, and might well have been astonished by the fact that the site of Cabin Hill much later became an enduring preparatory school.

Martha's more permanent return to Cabin Hill in the early years of the 19th century was encouraged by the upbringing and education of her nephew, Thomas, born to William and Sarah Drennan in March 1801. His parents sent him from Dublin to Belfast, where he was to reside almost permanently (along with his brother, William, born in 1802) until his premature death in 1812. Martha believed that the two boys benefited from the country air at Knock, and suggested to her brother in 1804 that "If your two boys get health and strength by Cabin Hill air, your £50 purchase money [which he had loaned in 1784] will be well-paid". William confided to his wife that he always regarded his sister as the dispenser of the most sage advice, and "in every real or supposed misfortune my best consoler and first friend".

The McTiers had sold part of the lease (17 acres) of Cabin Hill in 1789 ("a day of horror", Martha called it) to a Belfast businessman, Sam Hyde, who held it until his death ten years later. Martha regarded him as "a disgusting tyrant" towards his wife and found it hard to reflect upon his total indifference towards the estate for which she had so much affection; in April 1796 she returned to view it and complained that it was "now rising into full beauty without a single shrub being indebted to its present owner".

In 1800 a cousin of Martha, Martha Young, acquired the lease of Cabin Hill from Mrs Hyde, insisting that both parts of the divided property be reunited. She and another cousin, Ann Jane Bigger, then invited Martha to join them. Having considered the estate to be her "first-born", she re-discovered her lingering affection for the place: "surely, it is a dear little spot, in perfect neat order, both within and without – dairy-garden and meadow in rich abundance". Thereafter she divided her time between Belfast and Knock. She took an active and positive interest in the practical husbandry of the estate which produced fruit in abundance, and she sold hay to purchase cows; she defiantly boasted to her brother that "a garden, meadow, potatoes, and a patch of corn for one horse, is all in the farm, and I believe a woman might manage this without imposition or loss".

One of Martha's abiding memories from her earliest days at Cabin Hill had been "the note of the blackbird"; she felt that this encapsulated the charm and allure of the estate, and it as probably her sentiment which led her brother in 1815 to compose his poem, *The Blackbird at Cabin Hill*. When Martha Young died in 1807 she passed the lease to her cousin, who encouraged her brother to return to Belfast by handing the lease to him. William Drennan came to live in Cabin Hill, where he died in 1820. He was outlived for 50 years by his wife, who died in 1870 aged 99 or 100; Sarah's widowhood was of a similar length to that of Martha McTier who died completely blind in 1837. Some have suggested that, at 95 years of age, she may have been the oldest resident of Belfast. She was buried in Dundonald parish.

Legacy of the Scots

Martha believed that dishonesty was common amongst servants, but regarded them as no more nor less truthful than their superiors, and developed a good relationship with some of those at

Cabin Hill. The Marchioness of Donegall (whose Belfast residence was adjacent to that of Martha) once visited Cabin Hill, and this led to a friendship between her nephew, Thomas, and a footman of the Donegal household, which Martha did not discourage.

William Drennan had asked his sister to teach the young boy the correct pronunciation of words, and it is a testimony to a two-hundred-year legacy of the Scottish invasion of counties Antrim and Down that Martha observed in Thomas's accent, at two and a half years of age, "the true Caledonian twang of Belfast. In our kitchen they speak very ill, in the parlour only a degree better, so that his natural notes will soon be broad and harsh". This was less than two miles from the former centre of Gaelic power at Castlereagh.

E C S MEGAW

1908-1956

Eric Megaw had already developed a talent with early radio by the time he entered school. As a scholar, he picked up the first radio signal received in Ireland from New Zealand. In his professional career he made considerable advances in the use of radio waves, and was central to the development of radar just in time to deal with the threat of Hitler during the Second World War. He died suddenly from the stress of over-work.

Eric Megaw was born on 19 January 1908 at the Grand Hotel, Portobello in Dublin. He was the eldest of four sons of Arthur Megaw of north Belfast. All of the sons were educated at Campbell College, where Eric arrived in January 1922, already inspired by a book on electricity given as a birthday present, and versed in a theoretical and practical knowledge of radio waves which had been cultivated at Mourne Grange School. To facilitate his radio experiments, his father had built him a workshop at home – which, in scientific terms, merits all the mystique which has accrued, in literary lore, to the Little End Room of C S Lewis (see separate entry) at Belmont, only a mile from Campbell College. Eric was befriended by the Senior Science Master, Stephen Bennett (a well-known local botanist and President of the Belfast Naturalists' Field Club 1920-1922), who encouraged his youthful enthusiasm for home-made crystal sets.

The Merlin of the Wireless Society

Around April 1923 a Wireless Society was formed and young Eric addressed it on "various scientific aspects of wireless". It was boosted a year later by the establishment of the BBC in Northern Ireland. The Society quickly made a name for itself by relaying to the entire school a concert from Glasgow. This – somewhat surprisingly in an institution in which the Headmaster demanded mutual courtesy and good manners – elicited derision from a number of contemporaries, which gradually became endemic. Envy and cynicism led some to allege something more sinister and minatory in its arcane apparatus and esoteric language; there were references to an "exclusive and omnipotent cult" and "several fatuous-looking youths".

The coup which made Eric's reputation resulted from disobedience. As a boarder, he disregarded the school rules and constructed a wireless set under his bed, using the wire mattress as an aerial. In the very early hours one morning in 1923 he picked up the first verifiable radio message from New Zealand. When the news reached the press the Headmaster, 'Duffy' Gibbon, chose to ignore this infraction of the rules. Nevertheless, this led to a crescendo of irreverence: "I, for one, cannot feel anything but pity for this glorious being; for there is but one step between his glory and the mad-house", wrote one pupil, "Some day his brain will give way under the strain of imagination, and he will become a raving maniac. And that is what we in Campbell are faced with today – the prospect of the building being converted into a lunatic asylum".

Unfazed by this, and accepting it in good humour, he continued to pursue his obsession. In October 1924, whilst still a pupil, Megaw sent "the first radio signal transmitted by an amateur from Ireland on a set he had constructed himself. In the following year he established the first radio contact between Ireland and Australia", before forging, on 14 September 1925, the first link with the west coast of America.

Radio Waves

At Queen's University in 1926 Megaw worked with the Royal Geographical Society monitoring an Arctic expedition and operated an experimental short-wave radio on board the *Lord Antrim* en route to Montreal to investigate the possibilities of ship-to-shore radio. Upon graduation he became the youngest recipient of a Beit Fellowship at Imperial College in London which helped him to prepare for "his lifelong interest in the generation and application of very short length radio waves".

In 1930 he was employed at the General Electric Co (GEC) at Wembley where he continued to win awards, particularly for his work on the magnetron – a valve for very high frequency use which employs a magnetic field. In 1935 he was asked to demonstrate his own apparatus at public lectures given by two Nobel laureates associated with wireless transmission – Lord Rutherford and Guglielmo Marconi – who were both impressed.

In 1936 (whilst still with GEC) he was engaged by the Admiralty to work on valves and other electronic equipment, and became the leader of this team three years later. As there was a growing anticipation of war with Germany, his work became critical. A commission was formed in 1938 under the auspices of the Admiralty to hasten the development of microwave systems, and the first cavity magnetron was tested on 21 February 1940. Megaw and his team – who had been investigating a pulse transmitter suitable for short-wave airborne interception radar – were brought in to transform it into a workable design for airborne use and mass production. Megaw completed the design for the E1189 magnetron on 25 May 1940, and it first operated a month later. There are those who have argued that it was this, as much as anything – particularly after the loss of 173 bombers over England in early 1941 – which persuaded Hitler to abandon his planned invasion of England. Another Nobel Prize-winner who worked in the same field as Megaw, Sir Edward Appleton, later wrote that "the practical development of the cavity magnetron … was due to him. Yet, smilingly, he let the credit go wholly elsewhere". Megaw was awarded the MBE in 1943 for his achievement.

Post-war

The Irishman continued to serve on war-time radio committees, paying occasional visits to Northern Ireland, and travelling to North America for conferences in 1944. In January 1946 he was employed by the Royal Naval Scientific Service, being appointed its Director of Physical Research in 1950. In his final years he examined the links between scientific problems in astronomy, meteorology and radio, and his work on the theory of tropospheric forward scatter was published in May 1957 by the Institution of Electrical Engineering and posthumously granted its highest award. His sudden death, aged only 48, on 25 January 1956 was ascribed to the after-effects of rheumatic fever and the strain of over-work.

Family

His temperament was one of good humour and modesty, combined with natural talent; he could read and speak French, German and Italian. Despite all the vilification which he received at school, and the abstruse and often secretive nature of his work, as one friend recorded in an obituary in *The Times*: "He was no blinkered boffin, but a man of wide interests [particularly in poetry, literature and music] and good taste, with a civilised man's tolerance of people and views that were alien to him. He enjoyed the good things of life … Above all, he never allowed his intellectual preoccupations to dry up his generous and affectionate nature". Eric's Headmaster would have regarded that as a vindication of his own educational philosophy.

Eric Megaw married Therese Hija Veder of Amsterdam (who outlived him by about half a century) on 29 March 1933. They had two sons: the elder, Vincent (born 1934), became Professor of Archaeology at Leicester University and later at Flinders University in Adelaide, Australia; the younger, Edgar (born 1942) became Director of the Ergonomic Information Analysis Centre at the University of Birmingham. Megaw had three younger brothers, one of whom died relatively young. Arthur Hubert Stanley Megaw became Director of Antiquities in Cyprus, and Basil Richardson Stanley Megaw became an archaeologist and Director of the Manx Museum. Eric and his surviving brothers organised and attended their parents' Golden Wedding anniversary in September 1955 in Belfast, the last occasion on which he returned home.

His wife was the recipient of some affectionate and laudatory tributes to her husband. One of his colleagues noted that "he was able to make contributions of the highest importance to the future of the Navy". Appleton added: "The wrench is so terrible for many, especially for those people at the Admiralty who found him the perfect chief, stimulating, sympathetic, considerate, good-humoured – but all the time insisting on the highest standards in both work and conduct. You will understand how tragically I regard your husband's loss in the circle of British science". A memorial plaque was erected at the Ashby Institute of Queen's University.

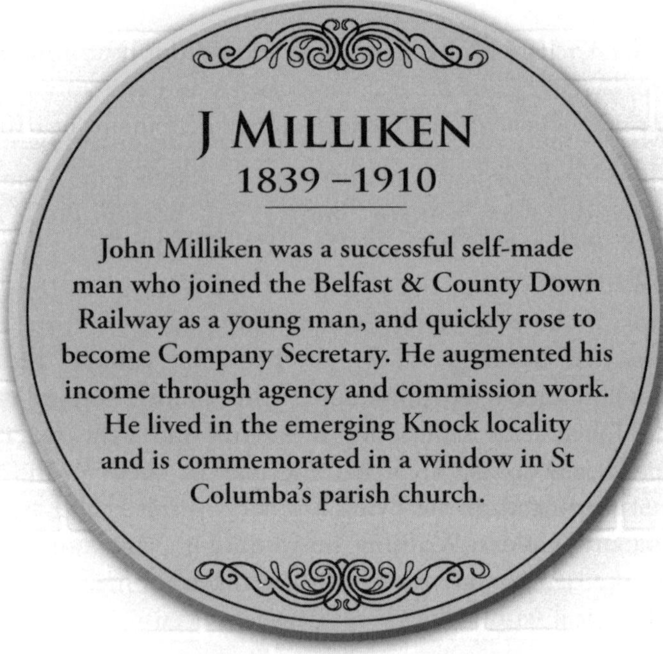

John Milliken was one of those individuals who earned financial and social respectability as a result of his own efforts and talent. He was born in August 1839 at White Park in Edendarriff, a townland of 551 acres close to Ballynahinch and Dromara. The district boasted a corn mill and, a decade after John Milliken's birth, an L-shaped bleaching factory was built by Hugh Milliken – probably his father – said to be the largest premises at that time in Co Down.

John's first position was at William Ewart & Son (probably in Belfast). In November 1862, he applied for a position as bookkeeper with the Belfast & County Down Railway (BCDR) at Queen's Quay in Belfast. He lost out to an applicant named Turkington, but reliable bookkeepers appear to have been hard to find. Turkington had himself replaced an errant employee named Goodwin but, after only six months, Turkington defaulted to the tune of £37, and Milliken finally took his opportunity. He was taken on at the age of 22 or 23 as a cashier and accountant at £80 per annum, which was set to rise in annual increments to £100. He found a guarantor for his employment in the shape of his uncle, James Kennedy of Rosetta (south-east Belfast), who was married to Agnes Milliken (Hugh's sister), who posted a very substantial security of £1000.

Company Secretary

The indications are that John Milliken took little time to display his flair for the commercial and business world, as he was quickly appointed Assistant Secretary, and then in 1867 – within four years of starting with the BCDR, with an annual salary of £200 – Company Secretary, a post he held until his resignation in 1895. Whilst prestigious, the position lacked glamour. Milliken was required to deal with awkward and aggressive customers which included fellow bookkeepers, such as a Mr Murray of John Arnott & Co. The latter was prosecuted in January 1882 by the BCDR for failing to pay the requisite fare for his dog, which resulted in Murray sending to the Company Secretary what the latter described as "a very unbecoming letter". A decade earlier John Milliken had been required to co-ordinate the Company's defence of, and response to, the rail accident that occurred close to Ballymacarrett Junction on the evening of Saturday 13 May 1871, which resulted in the death of two young passengers and injuries to thirty other people.

A photographic tribute in the *Belfast Evening Telegraph* at the time of his death described him as a "popular secretary", and one obituary asserted that customers of the BCDR "appreciated his courtesy and geniality no less than his employers did his fidelity and zeal". In 1875 the Directors specifically testified "in the strongest manner [to] their appreciation of Mr Milliken's services as Secretary and his attention to the interests of the Company at all times".

Nevertheless, the management of the railway company proved pedantic and, when Milliken's surety – James Kennedy – died in June 1879, he was required to obtain a replacement guarantor of his good conduct. The BCDR rarely produced good profits or dividends, and it may be a consequence of this that caused the company to say to Milliken when it granted him a £25 annual increment in December 1881 that: "he must consider [it] final, at least for some considerable time to come".

It may have been such circumstances which encouraged John Milliken to expand his financial interests by taking on company agencies. In October 1880, the BCDR Minutes reveal that he had been permitted to accept the agency of the Scottish Provincial Assurance Co, and during the following year he started to take leaves of absence ranging from a few days up to three weeks at a time. At the time of his death he was the representative for Guardian Assurance and – no doubt taking advantage of his professional connections – also for Johnson Cammell & Co of Sheffield which manufactured iron rails and wheels for British railways (which had amalgamated in 1903 to become Cammell Laird & Co).

Knock Resident

At the time of the rail accident in 1871 John Milliken, who was a Freemason, lived at 58 Pakenham Place on the Dublin Road. By 1877 he resided in the more residential suburb of Knock, sharing a house named Brenthamville with his sisters close to Knock BCDR station. When he married in November 1885 he moved to an adjacent house named Rüdesheim – still extant – on what is now the lower King's Road (although then known as Gilnahirk Road). He then purchased one of the first villas on the nearby Knockdene estate, newly developed on the site of an erstwhile nursery which dated back to 1841. Milliken's property – Astolat – is described in one source as "the most attractive of all the houses in Knockdene

– important as an early and striking example of the new architectural style which was to break away from the Victorian red brick tradition".

The growth of the district at the end of the 19th century persuaded Belfast City Council to search for a new cemetery, but the local residents were decidedly unenthusiastic about the prospect of such an intrusion in Knock. Milliken attended a disgruntled meeting with many others in Knock Presbyterian Church on 17 July 1896, and was part of a delegation to the Council in what is now the Old Town Hall five days later. They argued against a cemetery in the Knock area partly for sanitary reasons, but primarily on economic grounds. They were unhappy at the prospect of a potential 'double whammy' of increased taxes as a result of the recent encroachment of the city boundary, combined with the fact that a cemetery would cause a depreciation of the value of their recently-erected "villa residences". Milliken and his neighbours may have felt that the purchase in 1897 of the site of the current Dundonald Cemetery was a reasonable compromise.

The residential expansion of the Knock district at this time, however, necessitated the erection of three churches – Presbyterian, Methodist and Episcopalian. The occupant of Astolat appears to have been one of the prime movers behind the construction of the latter, St Columba's on King's Road (although originally named Church Road), for which the foundation stone was laid on 29 June 1895, with the consecration taking place almost exactly a year later on 13 June 1896. When Milliken moved to Bangor in June 1905 he was presented by an appreciative congregation with an illuminated address, which is now on display in the nave of St Columba's. It was drawn by John Milliken's celebrated neighbour, the artist J W Carey, who lived at Brugh, and features images of the church and Astolat, and also of a pastoral Knockbreda copied from an Andrew Nicholl painting. In language as florid as its polychrome decoration, which features two borders in medieval style, the document reads:

To John Milliken Esq.

Dear Sir

Your letter intimating that you were leaving Knock and that you had consequently resigned the office of the Honorary Secretary of St Columba's Church was received with sincere regret by the members of the General Vestry at their last Annual Meeting. It was then unanimously resolved that we could not allow you to part from us without some acknowledgement of the valuable services which you have rendered to our Parish since its inception. The result is this memento which we ask you to accept from the Congregation as a small token of their respect and esteem. We feel that it is a very inadequate recognition of your exertions to advance the interests of our Church, the success of which you have abundantly proved was one of your highest aspirations. Time, labour and material assistance you have always ungrudgingly given in helping to raise the Church to its present flourishing condition. Within your experience a small iron structure has been replaced by the present commodious and handsome building, and in the accomplishment of this noble work you have always evinced the greatest possible interest and have been ever willing to give a helping hand. Besides zealously and efficiently discharging the duties of Honorary Secretary, you have at various times filled other important offices including those of Churchwarden, Parochial Nominator and Synodsman. Further, the Diocesan Synod elected you as one of its representatives to the General Synod which we may call the Parliament of our Church. We wish you to remember that we shall always retain pleasant recollections of your fellowship with us and that we feel assured of your continued interest in our prosperity and progress.

The names attached included those of the minister, Rev Frederick William Austin, and the members of the congregation such as Dr Henry Norman Barnett (see separate entry), who lived at Thornhill and whose family gave its name to Barnetts Road; and John McCormick, Town Solicitor of Belfast, who lived at Craigroyston in Cherryvalley; and Frederick Hurley, a noted local photographer who lived at Beaconsfield on the Knock Road, now the site of the Marie Curie Hospice.

Final Years

John Milliken moved to Bayswater (where he made his will in September 1907) on Princetown Road in Bangor, where he was a member of the Royal Ulster Yacht Club. In October 1906 he purchased, for £2050 from the Land Commission, Oakley House – described in one source as "a great square mansion in the neo-classical style" – along with its nine acres in Holywood. It stood on the current site of Palace Barracks and was reputedly haunted. His marriage to Wilhelmina Seed Glenfield – at least fifteen years his junior – in early November 1885 was attended by colleagues from the BCDR, who presented him with a piano and dining room sideboard. After her death on 2 December 1904 (only six-teen days before the death of one of John's own sisters) he married Sara Gertrude Andrews. At the time of his death his address was given as East Hillbrook, a residence on what is now Victoria Road in Holywood.

He died, childless, after a six-week illness on the morning of 16 November 1910 at Erene Nursing Home at 2 Crescent Gardens close to Queen's University in Belfast. With perhaps inevitable irony, with Milliken having dealt with the aftermath of numerous rail accidents, minor and major, the *Belfast News Letter* reported a rail crash in England on the day of his death, in which a train driver and fireman were killed. He shared an obituary column with Count Leo Tolstoy. John Milliken was buried alongside his first wife in Clifton Street Cemetery, close to his parents, brother and a sister; another sister was later buried with them in 1937 (aged 95). His second wife, who died in Cheltenham on 4 March 1926, was awarded the OBE in June 1918 for her services as Lady Superintendent and Assistant Honorary Secretary of the Ulster Sphagnum Moss Association.

In the north aisle of St Columba's Church, the two outer frames of a triple window – representing Faith, Hope and Charity – are dedicated to John Milliken and his first wife (who was credited with the making of the Communion table linen for the inauguration of the church in June 1896).

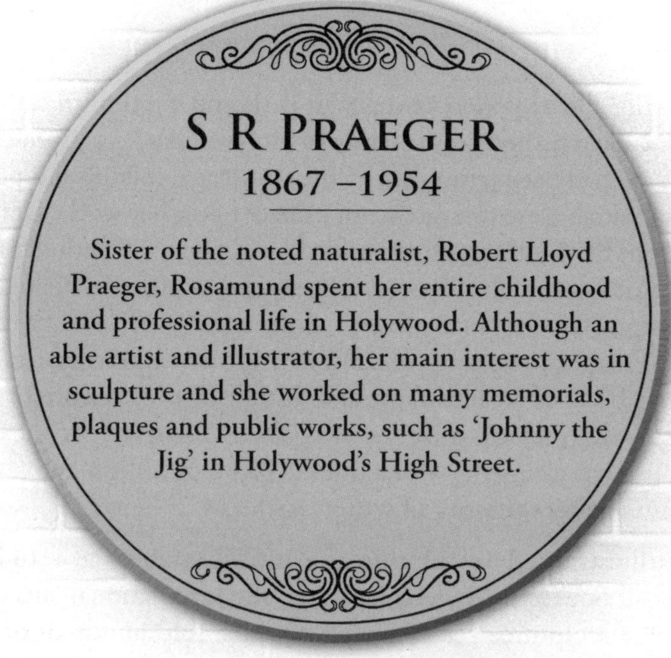

Rosamund Praeger – who owes her unusual name to her father's Dutch origins – was born in Holywood to where, after brief periods of study in London and Paris, she was to return permanently to live and work, and for which she retained a considerable affection. After her education at Sullivan Upper School, she attended the Belfast Government School of Art for two years from 1882, before continuing her interests and studies at the noted Slade School of Art in London, where she excelled. Another celebrated Ulster sculptor who was also trained at the latter was F E McWilliam who, as a pupil, will have witnessed the installation of some of Praeger's studio output at Campbell College between 1922 and 1923.

Studio

Following a brief period of study in Paris and a return to London, in 1892 she returned permanently to Holywood where, from childhood, she had been entranced by the landscape, folklife and people – all of which were to exercise an impact upon her work. Unlike a couple of her brothers who travelled to work in the United States, Rosamund never felt disposed to leave the locality. A catalogue of her output lists her first piece of work as a "portrait in chalk" in 1888. Financial necessity obliged her, in her earliest professional days, to become an illustrator and author of over a score of children's books (including *The Child's Picture Grammar*), as one commentator has claimed, "with a unique blend of realism and fantasy that anticipates the work of writers such as C S Lewis".

Primarily attracted to sculpting, she initially established a studio in Donegall Square in Belfast; however, the international success of her 1908 sculpture, *The Philosopher*, which sold hundreds of copies following its exhibition at the Royal Academy in 1913, enabled her to build her own St Brigid's Studio in Hibernia Street in her home town. She later carved a marble version of the little statue in 1920 and there are also bronze copies in the Ulster Museum and at Hunterhouse College. The last remaining copy of the original is now held in Holywood Library.

The catalogue of her output lists over 300 items exhibited between 1888 and 1951. Her earliest work was produced for the Belfast Ramblers' Sketching Club, but a large proportion was displayed by the Belfast Art Society and, in later years, at the Ulster Academy of Arts. Additionally, more than fifty works were shown at the Royal Hibernian Academy. These included drawings in various media, portraits, miniatures, tablets, memorials and sculptures. Her favourite amongst the latter, and consequently the most famous, is that in bronze of *Johnny the Jig*, which stands in Holywood High Street.

Memorials

Rosamund Praeger was also responsible for the production of a large number of memorials and plaques for notable Ulster characters. These include contributions to a number of War Memorials, and it was to cause considerable surprise that she was not asked to create the War Memorial for her home town. She was commissioned to provide a tablet for the Workman & Clark Shipyard First World War Memorial and in the Rosemary Street Presbyterian Church. She also carved the four statuettes – which represent Courage, Endurance, Life and Death – on the Campbell College memorial. It was typical of her affection for the local children that she used the young William Ferres as the model for her work. In 1915 she also painted a timely water-colour of Lieutenant Dermot Neill for his father, her neighbour in Holywood, the Donegall Place jeweller, Sharman D Neill. He lost both his sons during the War and the jeweller commissioned her to produce a memorial tablet to them in Holywood Presbyterian Church.

Other commissions in East Belfast included the carved stone font in Stormont Presbyterian Church. In the 1920s she worked on aspects of St Anne's Cathedral, including carvings in the baptistery and on the buttress capitals. In 1932 her William Reeves Memorial was added to the Cathedral, but her most famous contribution to its decoration was probably the 1938 plaque of Lord Carson. Praeger, in fact, created a multitude of similar memorials as St Patrick's Church in Jordanstown; to the naturalist and photographer Robert Welch in the Ulster Museum; to Thomas Andrews of *Titanic* fame; and to Rev Thomas Hamilton at Queen's University, which also holds her memorial to the sisters who founded Riddell Hall.

Family

She also cast a bronze bust of her brother, the noted naturalist and botanist, Robert Lloyd Praeger, which is now in the National Gallery of Ireland in Dublin where he worked as a librarian in the National Library; a bust of her brother also graces Holywood Library. Like her brother, she was an active member of many organisations which included the Belfast Rambler's Sketching Club, the Belfast Naturalists' Field Club and the National Trust. Numbered amongst her friends and acquaintances were Robert Welch, another photographer A R Hogg, and the artists Paul Henry and John Carey (whose brother and family lived at Brugh on Knockdene estate at Knock junction).

Following her mother's death in 1930 she sold the family home, Derryquin, and moved to Rock Cottage at Craigavad, where her brother joined her in the early 1950s before his death on 5 May 1953. She followed him to the grave on 17 April 1954, two days after her 87th birthday and was buried in the family plot (for which she had designed two figures: Hope and Memory) at Priory Cemetery in Holywood. She had sold the contents of her studio to the public in November 1952. This, combined with the nature of the casts and moulds that she used, has resulted in controversy in recent years, as her work became easy to replicate, and many fakes – which are often impossible to identify – have reached the market.

W H SMILES

1846 –1904

Yorkshireman William Smiles founded the Belfast Ropework Company at Connswater in 1875. He maintained its success in the face of numerous economic problems to make it the largest such factory in the world. He manufactured thousands of related products which he sold to over 100,000 customers, and employed over 3000 workers. The father of eleven children, he died suddenly at his golf club.

William Holmes Smiles is the subject of a disappointing entry in the recently published *Dictionary of Irish Biography* (2009) that does not do justice to the man who founded and developed the Belfast Ropework Company, which became the largest manufacturer of its type in the world.

Like his fellow Belfast entrepreneur, Edward Harland, Smiles was a Yorkshireman. His father, Samuel – who became celebrated as the author of the Victorian classic, *Self Help*, and who included a chapter on Harland in his *Men of Invention and Industry* – moved from the centre of Leeds in 1846 to Woodhouse on the northern outskirts of the city and thus avoided the typhus fever outbreak of 1847. William – the elder of two sons, who also had three sisters – was born in Woodhouse on 26 January 1846. When William was still young, the family moved to Blackheath near London where, in 1863, Samuel Smiles built a new family home (in the foundations of which he buried a copy of *Self Help*) named Westbank. The house-warming party took place on William's eighteenth birthday and, a few years later, he was to bestow its name on his own family home in Palmerston Road in Sydenham in east Belfast.

William was educated at King's College School in London, of which one school report (perhaps the final one) described him as "very practical and shrewd, yet not without a certain vein of sentiment and enthusiasm ... Clear-headed with much judgement, yet hasty, impulsive and somewhat opinionative". To some extent, this summary was later echoed by his daughter, Aileen, who stated that he was "small, determined and always sure he knew best".

Belfast

William joined the East India merchant company of Harvey, Brand & Co in 1862, at the age of sixteen, selling tea. He arrived in Belfast six years later as the firm's representative. In his early days in the town he appears to have taken ground floor lodgings in the Knock district. In 1870 he formed a partnership with W B Lowson, adding insurance to the tea trade. During the following year he purchased a half-share with Samuel Wilson in the small Ballymacarrett ropewalk of John Davidson (located on New Road, later the Newtownards Road), in which he also employed his younger brother, Samuel.

Lowson – who was at first much admired by Samuel Smiles senior, but who later came to be regarded as a rogue – eventually dissolved the partnership, and in 1875 William pursued a more ambitious project, forming a limited company called the Belfast Ropework Company. He was one of four Directors, who included William's own brother-in-law, Jack Hartree, and his friend from Strandtown, Gustav Wolff. The ambitious nature of the company is reflected in its description as early as 1877 in the *Belfast Trades' Directory* as twine and rope-makers, sailmakers, shipriggers and ships' chandlers. A preliminary Directors' meeting was held on 14 September 1876, at which – setting the tone for William Smiles's future imperturbable dedication to the firm – it was agreed that he would also act as Secretary *pro tempore* (in the event until 30 November), and would sign all the company's documents, bills and cheques.

William's brother, Samuel – who, in common with his father, was to hold shares in the Company – was never enamoured of the rope-making trade and, primarily as a consequence of the urging of his father, focused on the tea trade. In the late 1870s Samuel Smiles junior lived jointly at Derby Terrace in Strandtown with John McIntyre, of McIntyre & Osborne, wholesale tea agents, with whom Samuel probably worked. He eventually left Belfast, possibly around 1880.

Both brothers married in 1874 and, as William's second daughter (Aileen) later revealed, they settled in Strandtown "close to the railway station, the foreshore, the slob, the bathing boxes and each other". William developed close and enduring friendships with his neighbours, including the Heyns (of Strandtown House), the Jaffé family, Rev Thomas Hamilton of St Mark's Church, Gustav Wolff and Edward Harland. William, his daughter later claimed, "courted so many [women]", including Harland's sister-in-law, Anne Wann; however, he married Lucy Dorling – herself the half-sister of Isabella Beeton, the Victorian cookery celebrity – whom he had known since childhood, at St Saviour's Church in Pimlico, and took her on honeymoon to the Continent.

In the early days of their marriage they enjoyed a number of Sydenham addresses. William's own address in 1870 is given as Seaview, Strandtown. His family home in 1877 was Strandforeland Terrace – the forerunner of Palmerston Road – but he resided briefly around 1880 at Brandon Tower in the Connsbrook locality. The mania for organisation and self-discipline which plagued William Holmes Smiles all his working career may have been partly necessitated by the arrival of a large brood. His father, ironically, "had at first protested against the ever-increasing family in Belfast", asserting that he was trying Lucy too far – but such virility was almost a family tradition: Samuel Smiles was himself one of fourteen siblings, and he had sired five children. William and Lucy raised eight sons and three daughters at the affectionately-named Westbank on Palmerston Road.

Knowing the Ropes

On his marriage certificate (25 April 1874), even before the official foundation of the Belfast Ropework Company, William described himself as a 'ropemaker'. It was a trade at which he ultimately excelled. By the 1930s the company was spread over forty acres along the Connswater River – it was claimed that a man could cover seven miles of ropewalk without retracing his steps – and boasted an alleged 100,000 customers world-wide. The company initially employed 50 workers, but this total had risen to 800 within a decade; by 1888 there were one thousand workers on its books, then 2000 by 1892 and – with the opening of a new Mill in 1899 – the total reached in excess of three thousand. At the turn of the century, a contemporary newspaper feature suggested that "we are warranted in stating [that the Works] are the largest of the kind in the world".

The origins of the Belfast Ropework Company were very much as a subsidiary industry – a supplier to the shipping trade. This was partly reflected by the fact that Edward Harland was one of the earliest shareholders, as was his partner, Gustav Wolff – whose gothic script often penned the Annual Reports – who was also appointed Chairman. The earliest years were held hostage to a downturn in ship manufacturing. The 1877 Report noted "the depressed state of trade", echoed the following year when a slight loss was attributed to "The continued depressed state of the shipping trade, partly also to the fact that leading makers are adopting improved machinery". The 1879 Report lamented that: "the long continued depressed state of the shipping trade has had a natural influence on the ropemaking trade".

Nevertheless, it must be conceded that some of the financial difficulties of these years were compounded by poor commercial decisions. In 1878 there seemed to be the possibility of war with Russia, from where the Ropeworks acquired much of its hemp. The Board decided to ensure continued production by the purchase of the raw material at very high prices, but Disraeli returned with peace from the Congress of Berlin in mid-1878, and the price slumped – as one article in *The Belfast Telegraph* expressed it in March 1945 – "with dire results for the Ropeworks". During 1882 they installed new machinery in every department, but it was revealed at the Shareholders' meeting that the Company "has been crippled by accidents and delays". One of the problems that the Works faced was that it was on low-lying ground, and in early 1882 they had been flooded by unprecedented tides. Even in normal times it did not prove the most sanitary environment: during the Belfast Corporation enquiry in September 1896 into the state of public health there were complaints of "the volumes of steam emitted in the vicinity of the Ropeworks out of the distillery", which created an offensive smell. At that point, the Connswater River was regarded as essentially an open sewer.

The Company, however, demonstrated a remarkable resilience and capacity for expansion. In 1888 the Directors acknowledged the need for adaptability "owing chiefly to the change from sailing vessels to steamers; the consequence of this change [is that] the tendency of our trade for some years past has been to manufacture sundry smaller descriptions of cords, lines, twines, etc, and any increase in the Company's business has been in this direction". Overseas markets were tapped very early, and by the mid-1880s the Belfast Ropework Company was appointing agents to collect debts in the Ottoman Empire and the Kingdom of Greece. Such trade could create its own pressures, and in the first three years of the 1890s it had to report that political and economic uncertainties were having an impact upon trade in such diverse locations as the Argentine Republic and Australia. Nevertheless, it had won its first international medal in Sydney by early 1880, and won four more awards in the next three years. Share issues were taken up, with the result that by 1895 it was capitalised at £350,000, and at the turn of the century it could count 30,000 customers on its books. Such was its reputation that it was visited by Blondin, the celebrated tight-rope walker (although by then near-blind), who acquired some of the company's rope for his final public performance given in August 1896 in Belfast.

William Smiles the Businessman

William Holmes Smiles was appointed the first Managing Director of the Belfast Ropework Company – a post which he held until his death – and he was responsible more than anyone for the eventual success of the business. Upon his death, the *Belfast News Letter* justifiably described him as "all through, the presiding genius of the place, with its interests ever at his heart and always quick to seize any opportunity which would tend to improve its prospects and develop its trade".

At the turn of the century one assessment had claimed that: "The principles laid down in Dr Smiles's *Self Help* have a found a true and fitting expression in the busy and successful life of his worthy son". The irony was that William derided his father's commercial interpretation, describing the celebrated volume as "nothing but a collection of scraps"! Smiles senior offered a harsh assessment of poverty, which he attributed in many cases to "habitual improvidence"; he believed that the poor never benefited from periods of industrial prosperity, because the latter "were times in which publicans and beer sellers prosper and grow rich". It must have been in the general vicinity of the Ropeworks at Connswater that Corrie Chase (see separate entry) witnessed many idle men on street corners and in the doorways of public houses in the late 1920s – although some of such circumstances must have been the consequence of the gathering Depression.

William seems to have been of the opinion that a better appreciation of one's workforce literally paid dividends. One newspaper article observed that he had created spacious and well-appointed dining rooms at the Works "where they can obtain wholesome and nourishing meals at a cheaper rate than they could possibly be prepared in their own homes", and he extended the facilities when they proved inadequate after the construction of the new Mill in 1899. His readiness to acknowledge the vital role of his workers is reflected in a comment in the *Belfast News Letter* in its tribute to him at the time of his death:

> *He was indeed one of those captains of industry to whose enterprise and foresight the growth of our city and its commercial progress must to a large measure be attributed though, as no-one would have more readily admitted than himself, the efforts of such leaders would have been comparatively useless without the skill and perseverance of their hardworking workpeople.*

As Managing Director Smiles was paid, in 1882, £700 per annum plus "one-fourth of net profits of the Company beyond 10% per annum"; by 1895 his remuneration was £1750 per annum plus one-twentieth of the profits. The affluence and prosperity of most of the late 19th century Belfast enterpreneurs seems to exude an air of inevitability. The contemporary press was at best deferential and at worst adulatory about their talent for garnering wealth, and the commercial legerdemain of some of them was almost apotheosised. Pirrie lived by a book of eclectic maxims given to him by his mother which helped to channel the wealth-gathering ethic. William Holmes Smiles adopted a more pragmatic approach, but he also kept a commonplace book of press cuttings which included amusing anecdotes and mundane philosophy, one of which best adumbrated his personal approach to business:

> *Wealth is not acquired, as many persons suppose, by fortunate speculations and splendid enterprises, but by the daily practice of industry, frugality and economy – he who relies upon these means will rarely be found destitute, and he who relies upon any other will generally become bankrupt.*

His dedication to the company was little short of obsessive, so much so that his eldest son – John Holmes Smiles – joked that it was the Ropeworks which was truly his 'eldest son'. A daughter, Aileen, echoed this in commentary upon the influence of her grandfather, Samuel Smiles senior, had upon William's work ethic:

> *Willy, the rope son, resembled his father too closely for any comfort. Work, which for the father was a predilection, became with the son a mania. I can still hear Willy (my father) hissing through his teeth in alarming fashion at my eight brothers, who did not make work their God. Work! Work! Do you want your mother to keep you, sir? Do you want your sisters to keep you?*

Living within a mile of the Connswater complex he appears to have developed some kind of symbiosis with the plant. He was a constant worrier, and his daughter claimed that: "He would dream that it was on fire. Indeed one night he rose from his bed and rushed down to Connswater to find the ropery really was alight". His wife admitted that he would lay awake most of the night pondering business matters; he woke her up one night saying that he was certain something was amiss at the Works. He ignored her protestations, and "arrived there about 4 am ... in time to stop a lorry load of rope being stolen".

Throughout his entire career he rarely missed a Board meeting. Apart from absences for commercial reasons, he was reluctant to be away from Connswater. A minute of 13 March 1889 recorded that:

> *A further conversation took place with reference to effecting such arrangements, by appointing a general assistant, as would enable Mr Smiles to take longer holidays in the future than he has enjoyed in the past. Mr Smiles explained very fully the complete system he had established throughout the Works and offices which rendered his constant oversight not absolutely necessary.*

This practical approach to management served the company well when he died suddenly in 1904. Viscount Pirrie at Harland & Wolff proved to be the managerial equivalent of the gravitational black hole – absolutely no matter escaped his orbit as Chairman. The *Belfast News Letter* expressed it benevolently when it wrote that Pirrie had "complete confidence in himself and in the schemes which were evolved in his marvellous brain" – but he shared none of them and, in the event of his unexpected death in 1924, Pirrie's ruthless and secretive singularity left both the shipyard and his wife in parlous financial circumstances.

A company from Leeds despatched their sympathy to Smiles's wife: "We learned to appreciate and respect his absolute integrity, uprightness and honour in all business transactions as much as in private life", and his colleagues expressed the same, if lengthier, sentiments. Tributes from close and beholden associates are often an opaque source of truth, but the Directors of the Belfast Ropework Company were probably sincere and accurate when they penned their epitaph on his near-30-year contribution to the company:

> *Practically its founder, he devoted his whole time and ability to its service, and it has been largely owing to his energy and capacity that the splendid position of the Company is due. Personal considerations or his own convenience were never allowed by him to interfere with*

what he considered was for the interests of the Company. Self was completely extinguished in duty. Strictly just at all times with the staff and the workers, he always evinced the greatest care and consideration for their comfort and happiness. Himself of the highest integrity and honour, he inculcated the same principles on all who served under him, so that now the Company's reputation for fair dealing is of the highest and forms an item of great value in its goodwill.

William Smiles the Family Man

Religion and politics do not appear to have unduly troubled the routine of the businessman. Although he adopted the standard anti-Home Rule stance, he rarely engaged in political debate; and, although Westbank was a very short walk to St Mark's Church on the Holywood Road, his only regular attendance at church was said to be for the christening of his children. Nevertheless, despite his dedication to his commercial career, he made time for family and relaxation, his principal passion being golf. He was a founder member of Royal County Down Golf Club in Newcastle; he was one of the original members, and one-time captain, at Royal Belfast Golf Club at Kinnegar in Holywood; and was also a member at the Royal Portrush club.

Most, if not all, of his eight sons, attended Rossall Prep School in Lancashire, and surviving letters suggest that he took some effort to show an interest in their education. One of the sons, Alan, did occasionally ask why his father did not write more often, but took the opportunity to ask for "foreign stamps from the Ropeworks".

There are incidental hints of the imposition of Victorian discipline. One source reveals that, presumably when all his children were old enough, he led all thirteen members of the family on a regular Saturday afternoon bicycle ride on an invariable route from Westbank to Newtownards, Bangor and Donaghadee. Smiles's own parents also visited Belfast regularly, as Samuel Smiles senior attended the OGM of Ropeworks' shareholders to hear the annual dividend. Aileen Smiles recalled that all fifteen of them could occasionally be spotted walking "along the White Rocks sands at Portrush ... an army of us children walking uncomfortably in our little boots because it was Sunday and we were not allowed to wear our sand-shoes. Mother with her stick drawing all the children's names in the sands".

William's eldest son, John Holmes Smiles, was to be appointed an interim joint-Manager of the Ropeworks upon his father's death. He was the only one of his brothers to sign the Solemn League & Covenant against Home Rule in September 1912, and did so at Westminster, London. His mother and second sister, Aileen, both signed the Declaration – the female equivalent – at St Mark's Church. One son, Captain Alan Smiles was killed instantly by a shell on 9 July 1916 during the Battle of the Somme, and is commemorated on the iconic Thiepval Memorial. His brother, Samuel – who returned from a legal position in Buenos Aires to enlist – perished on 16 August 1917 during the Battle of Passchendaele, and lies buried in the largest Commonwealth military cemetery at Tyne Cot, east of Ypres (now known as Ieper).

Another younger brother, Lieut-Colonel Sir Walter Dorling Smiles, enjoyed a notable military and political career. He represented constituencies at Westminster and Stormont, and drowned on The *Princess Victoria* off the coast of Donaghadee on 31 January 1953. His daughter, Patricia Ford (Lady Fisher), became the first woman MP to take her seat at Westminster, and later succeeded to her father's Stormont seat. She was the grandmother – and thus William Holmes Smiles was the great-great-grandfather – of the television explorer Bear Grylls. Another grand-daughter, whom William never knew, was the novelist, biographer, sports' journalist, radio actress, television game-show star and Fleet Street journalist, Nancy Spain (died 1964), the daughter of William's youngest daughter, Norah.

Dr Samuel Smiles was to outlive both his sons – Samuel junior died in 1903 – and two of his three daughters. He survived William by three months, dying at the age of 91. On Saturday 9 January 1904 William Holmes Smiles took the train to Newcastle to play golf. He died in the changing rooms at 2 pm, a fortnight short of his 58th birthday, as his daughter later wrote: "already worn out by rope and children". His body was returned to Belfast on the 6.35 pm train. On the following day the entire congregation at St Mark's rose as a mark of respect as the organ played the melancholic 'Dead March' from Handel's *Saul.* Ten shillings were paid to open the grave at Belfast City Cemetery following 'a strictly private' funeral on the Tuesday. It was a tribute to his management style that, as the cortège travelled under the Holywood Arches and passed by the entrance of the Belfast Ropework Company on the Newtownards Road, "There was no stoppage of work ... the machines were going full tilt. Only a yard man, hat in hand, stood at the gate to pay homage".

William had made his will only three months earlier on 5 October 1903. His wife, Lucy, who was to live to the age of 91, was to be allowed to stay in Westbank as long as she wished. William bequeathed to her the standard contemporary legacy, which included his watches, jewels, ornaments, plate, furniture, linen, glass, pictures, musical instruments, horses, carriages, saddlery, stable furniture, and household stores and provisions, and even any live and dead stock – plus an immediate payment of £500. The Directors of his creation were equally generous sending, along with their sincere tribute, a cheque for £875. One suspects that, in common with so many wealthy widows, she would probably have preferred a few more years of her husband's personal companionship.

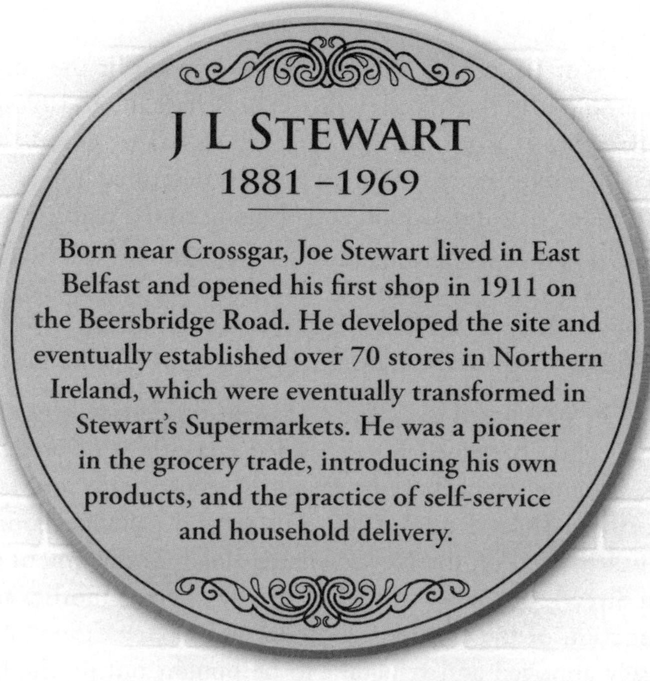

If you approach the Knock junction from the direction of Stormont and turn left on to the dual carriageway, you are effectively passing through what once was the living room (at 2 Knock Road) of Joseph Lowry Stewart. As with his home – demolished to accommodate the projected widening of the road – all traces of his business empire in Northern Ireland have now been eradicated.

Entrepreneur

Joe Stewart was born on 11 December 1881 in the townland of Creevycarnonan near Crossgar, where his father, Hugh (in company with other relations), was a farmer. Joe, his brother and three sisters appear to have sprung from hardy stock, as they all survived into their 80s and 90s.

At the age of 14 he was apprenticed to a grocer at the corner of Cromac Square in the Markets district of Belfast and in 1903 joined the Agnes Street store (off the Shankill Road) of grocer George Kelly, whose reference in 1908 for Stewart described him as "a very honest, sober, truthful, careful and obliging young man". After two brief spells of work in Canada, Joe Stewart opened his own grocery store – Greenville Cash Stores – with a fanfare of publicity on 30 September 1911, at 9 Greenville Terrace (alternatively: 334 Upper Beersbridge Road) in the Bloomfield district of East Belfast.

In 1922 he purchased two of the adjacent properties, plus another in 1927, and christened his expanded emporium Stewart's Cash Stores, a name which became instantly recognisable and familiar in Northern Ireland until 1969. His second principal long-term store was located on the Newtownards Road (at the junction with Gawn Street), but in 1916 he had briefly opened another store at the junction of the Castlereagh Road and Isoline Street, and was intensely annoyed and reluctant to be bought out by the Co-op. He vowed that thereafter he would open a rival establishment close to any new Co-op store which opened. He kept his word, and eventually boasted 72 shops throughout Northern Ireland.

Whilst his name is not as celebrated as that of other businessmen of East Belfast – such as Lord Pirrie and Sir Edward Harland (of Harland & Wolff), and Sir Samuel Davidson (the founder of Sirocco Works) – Stewart's entrepreneurial flair bears comparison with theirs. He ran a successful commercial enterprise which, based in East Belfast for over eighty years, provided employment for many thousands (in 1986 the company boasted 3000 employees). His approach to business echoed the advice which Pirrie accepted from his own mother: "You have your own way to make; it depends of your exertions whether you succeed or not".

Joe Stewart was a grocer who was fastidious about the details of his trade. Even during his second honeymoon in 1936, and on a holiday the following year to North America, he visited several bakeries to evaluate new trends and ideas. Like Harland and Davidson, the man from Crossgar displayed a creative and pioneering spirit. He made his own bread, initially above the Greenville store; however, it became so popular that in 1929 he had to build a new bakery on the adjacent Greenville Road. His Tip-Top bread eventually became better known as (the still extant) Sunblest loaf. To cope with demand for his cheap butter, he installed the first automatic weighing and wrapping machine in the province. One concept from North America which he introduced to his shops was that of self-service; this was first employed at his store on Cregagh Road (now Tesco's) – the only disadvantage was that it operated a one-way system and, if you missed an item, you had to go round and queue again!

He obtained a good price for the produce he purchased in the markets because he bought in bulk and was able to offer cheaper prices to his customers. He constantly checked and assessed his competitors, and undercut their prices. The absolute principle by which he traded – as implied in the company name – was 'cash only', and this applied also to the home delivery service which he pioneered in the 1920s. No exceptions were permitted. It was a policy which indisputably worked and was consolidated by his personal reputation for honesty and integrity. During the Second World War he refused to entertain the offer of a contraband load of sugar from the Irish Free State, and annoyed his (second) wife by insisting that any of their butter ration which had not been used should be returned to the Government.

Employer

Joe Stewart was a notoriously demanding employer – no-one was allowed to sit in his stores even during lengthy shifts – but he asked nothing of his employees which he did not perform himself. When

Thomas Andrews (later designer and victim of the Titanic) obtained a premium apprenticeship at Harland & Wolff, his uncle Lord Pirrie made it clear that no favours would be shown to him and stipulated that "by his own efforts and abilities he must make his way". Joe Stewart adopted the same philosophy. At various times, he employed a number of his own children and extended family, but none of them was shown preference, and none of them rose to a permanent, prominent position in the company.

Despite this exigent manner, he remained a popular employer and, following a brief resignation in 1944 after a disagreement, his prompt return was greeted by his delighted employees with the presentation of a commissioned illuminated address. Some staff served the company for very lengthy periods, sometimes in excess of forty years. Individuals were able to aspire to the Board Room from the lowliest of starts. Hugh Shaw from East Belfast started as a shelf-filler in 1928, and retired after 51 years of service having been a Director and General Manager. James Laverty Boyd, who became Chairman and Managing Director, had served 60 years by 1984. In the south aisle of St Columba's Church of Ireland on King's Road there are two stained-glass windows dedicated to himself and his wife, Edna Thomson Boyd.

Reluctant Retirement

In 1935, Joe Stewart sold Stewart's Cash Stores to Weston's, the Canadian international grocery business, which effectively made him a millionaire. He had, however, no other passions in life beyond the grocery trade and was retained by the company. So traumatic was any prospective departure to him that, when he reached 70, the company removed his name-plate from his office door as a hint that he was being retired! He spent some of his subsequent years assisting his son, Jack, to run Loughview Nurseries at Gilnahirk. In 1969, the year of Joe Stewart's death, the company name and philosophy was changed to Stewarts' Supermarkets, and by the late 1990s it had been absorbed by the ever-expanding Tesco's, which unsympathetically and tragically destroyed eighty years of company history and paraphernalia.

On 16 January 1911 Joe Stewart married Cassie (Catherine) Christie, by whom he had two sons and a daughter. Following her death in December 1934 as a result of cancer, he married one of his employees, Rose Chisholm Hill, on 24 September 1936 at St Martin in the Fields at Trafalgar Square. She provided him with another son and daughter. After initially living at Wingrove Gardens in the Bloomfield area, Joe Stewart occupied a number of addresses – including Rosepark at Dundonald and Circular Road in Belmont – until he bought no.2 Knock Road upon his enforced retirement.

He succumbed to a short illness and died on 27 October 1969, just short of his 88th birthday. To the end he manifested his tight management skills, by interfering as little as possible with normal shopping hours. He was buried at Dundonald Cemetery on the afternoon of Wednesday 29 October – when the shops were on half-day closing!

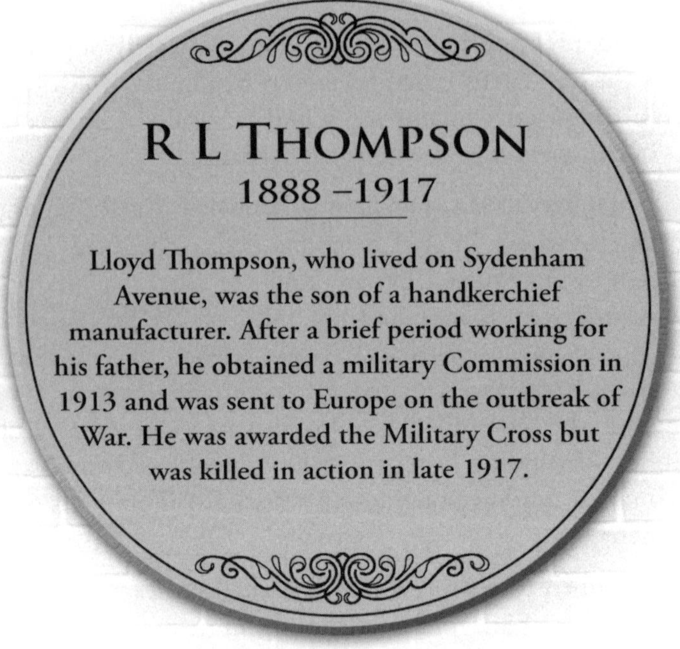

Lloyd Thompson's first name was given in honour of his maternal grandfather, the Rt Hon Robert Thompson, who ran his own company, Lindsay Thompson & Co, which boasted two mills in Belfast, making a living from weaving, flax and thread manufacturing. He was MP for North Belfast from 1910 and Chairman of the Belfast Harbour Commissioners from 1907, until his death on 3 August 1918 at his residence, Bertha House on the Malone Road. (The latter had also previously been the home of Alfred Squire Taylor, an Irish rugby international who was killed at Ypres during the First World War).

The businessman-cum-politician sired four sons and five daughters. One of his sons was Samuel Herbert Hall-Thompson who lived at Netherleigh on Massey Avenue (which was then serviced only by a cesspool) from 1921 until he sold it to Campbell College in the late 1920s. He returned to Netherleigh in 1944 as

Minister of Education, working from his former bedroom. Two of Robert Thompson's daughters rather confusingly married men named Thompson. Sara(h) Thompson married James Armstrong Thompson, who established his own cambric handkerchief and fancy linen business in Hope Street, off Sandy Row.

The latter's family residence was Penrhyn at the junction of Belmont Church Road and Sydenham Avenue. The Thompsons enjoyed a sociable relationship with other local residents such as the Lewis and Greeves families and in October 1916 C S Lewis, then at school in Surrey, was despondent that he could not accompany his friend Arthur Greeves from Bernagh (later known as Red Hall on Circular Road) on a visit to Penrhyn.

Artilleryman

Early in 1905 Lloyd Thompson, the only son of James Armstrong Thompson, started work for his father. He obtained a Commission (as 2nd Lieut) in the RFA Special Reserve in 1913, and was called to active service in August the following year. During the following month he was sent with the BEF to the continent and at some time around the end of November 1914 he wrote to Campbell College indicating that he had "just been moved to the Brigade Ammunition Column, which is the last stage before going into a battery". The same correspondence articulates the early impact which the European conflict had upon the locality, as he noted the early death of three of his school friends, including Henry Ouseley Davis who had served on the HQ Staff of the UVF at Craigavon House during the Home Rule Crisis (and to whom there is a memorial plaque in the parish church of his home town, Holywood).

Soon after this Lloyd Thompson was attached to 86 (Howitzer) Battery, a unit of 12 (Howitzer) Brigade in the RFA. On 9 June 1915 he wrote from the Front to admit that "So far we have been very fortunate; although in a bad place, we have had comparatively few casualties. The gas has been rather a trouble ... [The British Tommy has been getting] wet and cold for four or five days at a time, many getting frost-bitten. I saw some of the happiest faces amongst those on their way to hospital ... When I left the old school little did I ever expect to take part in a war against the greatest foe civilisation has ever known". At that stage 86 Battery appears to have been disbanded, and Lloyd Thompson was transferred to 'C' Battery in 173 Brigade RFA, as part of 36 (Ulster) Division. Divisional artillery – which, in military terms, might be termed 'a movable fist' – had originally been created for the Ulster Division in London, and 172 and 173 Brigades were raised in North London, and known respectively as the East Ham and West Ham units.

The move coincided with Thompson's promotion on 17 June 1915 to the rank of Lieutenant. His courage and professionalism elicited favourable comment; his Colonel wrote: "as a battery commander a more able and energetic officer he never wished to have. [Thompson] was splendid in every way". At some unspecified point in 1915 – probably after June, as he does not mention his injuries in his letter – he was severely injured and invalided home, and was also mentioned twice in despatches. On 14 January 1916 he was gazetted as a recipient of the Military Cross, with which he was personally decorated by King George V. The erstwhile linen merchant was engaged in the Somme campaign in July 1916, and at Messines one year later, when his battery was ordered across No Man's Land, establishing themselves as far forward as the Red Line.

A few months later on 20 November 1917 Thompson, who by this stage had been promoted to the rank of Major, was engaged with his battery in trying to capture German trenches during the Battle of Cambrai, in a position just south of the Bapaume-Cambrai road and on the western bank of the Canal du Nord. There had been a great movement of guns in preparation for what one source described as "a staggering artillery duel". 173 Brigade was located east of the small village of Demicourt, and in the final days of the month was on the crest of Demicourt Hill, where the artilleryman was killed at an observation post on 1 December. His Brigadier-General wrote to Thompson's father that: "He had invariably carried out his duties with keenness and capacity. He was a great friend of mine, and I cannot tell you how I will feel his loss ... he was universally popular. I was up at the observation post very shortly after the sad event; he was unconscious from the moment he was hit and died almost immediately afterwards". An RAMC Captain confirmed his popularity: "The Major was esteemed the bravest man, the kindest and most lovable gentleman, endorsed not only by men of his own battery, but throughout the whole Division".

Robert Lloyd Thompson was thus outlived by both his grandfather and his father, who died tragically as a consequence of a fire in his bedroom at Penrhyn on 2 January 1952.

Memorials

Major Lloyd Thompson was buried only a short distance from Demicourt in plot I.A.4 of Hermies Hill British Cemetery which had been created only the previous month. A week after his death a meeting was held in his memory at the Rest House for Wounded Sailors and Soldiers which had only recently been established at the Commercial Hotel in Belfast. In 1919 James Armstrong Thompson and his wife erected a memorial window to their son in St Mark's Church on the Holywood Road, consisting of three lights depicting valour, sacrifice and love, and featuring the badge of the Royal Artillery, and an image of their son's Military Cross.

In addition to being listed on the War Memorial of the family church, Robert Lloyd Thompson is featured on those at Campbell College, QUB and in Strandtown. His name is also inscribed on the Thompson family headstone (plot H-474/5/6) at Belfast City Cemetery, where his uncle Samuel Hall-Thompson is also buried (plot G-600). A cousin, Robert Lloyd Hall-Thompson born in April 1920, later a member of the Parliament of Northern Ireland in 1969 and of the Northern Ireland Assembly in 1973, was named in memory of the deceased soldier. Lloyd Thompson died a bachelor and intestate, although his personal estate (administered by his father) totalled £439 12s 11d.

BALLYHAY BOOKS

For more information and to see our other titles, please visit our website
www.cottage-publications.com
or alternatively you can contact us as follows:-

Telephone: +44 (0)28 9188 8033
Fax: +44 (0)28 9188 8063

Ballyhay Books
is an imprint of
Laurel Cottage Ltd.,
15 Ballyhay Road,
Donaghadee, Co. Down,
N. Ireland, BT21 0NG